To Barbara & Rick,

Thanks for broadening my world of
wine, but more importantly, thank you
for your friendship & support!

Timothy Snider

6/20/17

THE FORTUNATE SON
TOP, THROUGH THE EYES OF OTHERS

by

TIMOTHY TRAINER

FOREWORD *by*

BARRY McCAFFREY, GENERAL
US ARMY (RET.)

· Chicago ·

THE FORTUNATE SON

TOP, THROUGH THE EYES OF OTHERS

by

TIMOTHY TRAINER

FOREWORD BY
BARRY MCCAFFREY, GENERAL US ARMY (RET.)

Published by
Joshua Tree Publishing
• Chicago •

JoshuaTreePublishing.com

13-Digit ISBN: 978-1-941049-72-3
Trade Paper: 978-1-941049-73-0
eBook: 978-1-941049-74-7

Disclaimer:

This book is designed to provide information about the subject matter covered. The opinions and information expressed in this book are those of the author, not the publisher. Every effort has been made to make this book as complete and as accurate as possible. However, there may be mistakes both typographical and in content. Therefore, this text should be used only as a general guide and not as the ultimate source of information. The author and publisher of this book shall have neither liability nor responsibility to any person or entity with respect to any loss or damage caused or alleged to be caused directly or indirectly by the information contained in this book.

Printed in the United States of America

DEDICATION

This work is dedicated to military brats. Military brats are rarely visible. Many are born into a life of sacrifice because your serving parent was elsewhere on a deployment or tour of duty. Sacrifice is something you do without knowing and, often, before you take your first step or speak your first word. In fact, for most, there is no sense of sacrifice because it is a way of life; you are born into it. You serve without being asked to serve. Some have and will sacrifice by experiencing the ultimate loss, the loss of a parent who served in harm's way because duty called.

Rest assured that you are not alone because there are thousands scattered throughout the country and around the world living on and around various army posts, naval, marine or air force bases and installations. Some of you take great pride in being called Army "brats" or Navy "brats" or whichever service applies. And, regardless of age or if you served in uniform, there is something special and different about being a military brat.

There may be times when you think that nothing makes up for those prolonged absences, absences on birthdays, Christmas, Thanksgiving, and other holidays, the day a younger brother or sister took his or her first step without that parent being there and other days that are significant in your lives. If you are fortunate, you may meet the men and women who served with your parent in harm's way and learn how much your sacrifice meant to them, having your parent at or near their side during some of the worst moments of their lives.

This book is dedicated to the tens of thousands of anonymous military brats, regardless of which branch of service applies. You have served and continue to serve. And, if you are as fortunate as I am, perhaps you will meet those who served with your serving parent during those very trying times and learn what your sacrifice meant to them and why it was, perhaps, more important that your parent was with them than with you.

Timothy Trainer

TABLE OF CONTENTS

THANKS AND APPRECIATION

I am indebted to numerous people who encouraged me to pursue this project and made it possible. There are those whose oral recollections of their tour of duty in Vietnam were simply recollections meant to be shared at reunions and gatherings, which I was privileged to attend.

Others who served with my father offered to participate and allowed me to record their recollections for this project. For those who have allowed me to record their recollections and our conversations, what has been provided allows their family members to crack the window open to their experience, their recollections, some of which may not have been shared before with spouses, parents, children, siblings, nephews or nieces. This project may have had in mind an intended focus on one person, but as you will read, it was important to tell, in no small part, the story of each person who participated in this project.

These recollections were invaluable to fulfill the aim of the primary reason for this project, but after hearing the experiences of everyone who participated, I hope that in some small way that what is told in the following pages contributes to a greater appreciation of what each of these men did in their youth. To their families, while it may not answer any questions, perhaps, it puts some things in perspective or allows them to take a moment to understand the men they are today.

The men who shared their experiences and made these pages possible served with my father. With the exception of one, all served in Bravo Company, 2nd Battalion, 7th Cavalry Regiment, 1st Air Cavalry Division, (B2-7), in 1968 and 1969. Their time together in B2-7 was, in some cases, a very short period of time.

MEN OF DIVISION, (B2-7) IN 1968 AND 1969.

Dale Beierman

Paul Decker

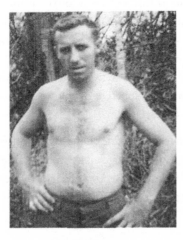

Rich Dorsey

Gerald "Jerry" Gast

THEN . . .

Their time together in B2-7 was, in some cases,
a very short period of time.

Jesse "Pops" Groves

Fred Hall

Edd Holtz

Jack Jeter

MEN OF DIVISION, (B2-7) IN 1968 AND 1969.

Jon "Snag" Johnson

Michael K. McMahan

Jack "Squirt" Miller

William "Bill" Montgomery

THEN . . .

Chris Sayre

Larry "Skinny" Spaulding

MONTHS SPENT IN B2-7

Year	JG	JJ	RD	DB	JG	M^2	WM	EH	J^2	LS	CS	PD	JM	ET	BM
4'68	X														
5'68	X														
6'68	X	X													
7'68	X	X	X												
8'68	X	X	X	X	X	X									
9'68	X	X	X	X	X	X	X	X	X						
10'68	X	X	X	X	X	X	X	X	X						
11'68	X	X	X	X	X	X	X	X	X	X	X	X	X	X	X
12'68	X	X	X	X	X	X	X	X	X	X	X	X	X	X	X
1'69	X	X	X	X	X		X	X	X	X	X	X	X	X	X
2'69	X		X	X	X		X	X	X	X	X	X	X	X	X
3'69	X		X	X	X		X	X	X	X	X	X	X	X	X
4'69	X		X	X	X		X			X	X	X	X		
5'69			X	X	X		X			X	X	X	X		
6'69			X	X	X		X			X			X		
7'69			X		X					X			X		
8'69										X					
9'69										X					
10'69										X					
11'69										X					

JG: Groves; JJ: Johnson; RD: Dorsey; DB: Beierman;
JG: Gast; M^2: McMahan; WM: Montgomery; EH: Holtz;
J^2: Jeter; LS: Larry Spaulding; CS: Sayre; PD: Decker;
JM: Miller; ET: Top; BM: McCaffrey

MAP OF VIETNAM

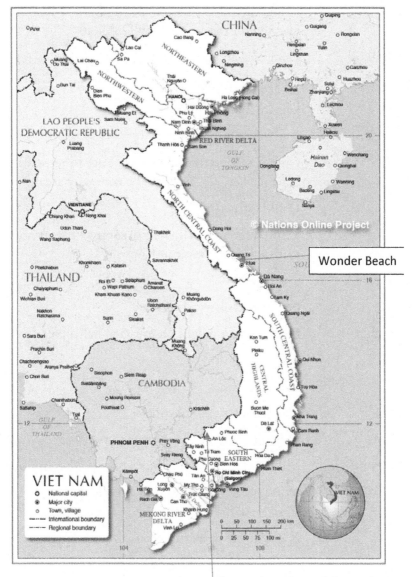

Wonder Beach

Approximate location of Quan Loi

ACRONYMS AND TERMINOLOGY

AIT	Advanced Individual Training
B2-7	Company B, 2nd Battalion, 7th Cavalry Regiment (element of the 1st Cavalry Division)
Battalion	Generally about 700 men (4+ companies)
Brigade	Generally made up of 3 to 5 battalions
CO	Commanding Officer
Company	consists of platoons, usually 4 ($\approx$120 men)
CQ	Charge of Quarters (overnight duty to respond to emergencies, etc., oversee the company area)
DI	Drill Instructor
EM	enlisted man (usually referring ranks E-1, privates, to E-4, below a sergeant)
Evac'd	evacuated
FAO	Forward artillery observer
Loach	nickname for a light observation helicopter
LP	Listening post
LZ	Landing Zone
M-16	Basic infantry assault rifle
M-60	Machine gun—belt fed general purpose
MOS	Military Occupational Specialty, job description
NCO	Non-commissioned officer, usually an E-5 (3-stripes) and higher
NDP	Night defensive perimeter
NVA	North Vietnamese Army

OCS	Officer Candidate School
Platoon	≈25 men, consists of squads, usually 4
RTO	Radio Telephone Operator
Shake 'n' Bake	term for Vietnam era buck sergeants (basic training, AIT, NCO school), becoming "instant" NCOs.
Six	Company radio short hand call sign for the company commander
Slick	a helicopter
Squad	10 or fewer make up a squad
Top	First Sergeant/Top ranking NCO in a company size unit

FOREWORD

Almost 50 years ago as an infantry Captain on my third combat tour, I took command of B Company, 2nd Battalion, 7th Cavalry in Vietnam (B2-7). I took command following the loss of their terrific young company commander, Captain William Meara, who was killed-in-action during a vicious close-range firefight. The battalion had just deployed south by Air Force C130s as part of an emergency movement from the northern I Corps Tactical Zone. We joined the entire 1st Cavalry Division (Airmobile) in a screening operation along the Cambodian border in III Corps Tactical Zone north of Saigon. Our mission was to fight a reconnaissance-in-force battle and fall back in zone blunting and slowing the expected NVA offensive. The enemy objective was to destroy the massive US Long Binh military logistics base.

We got our ass handed to us. The NVA were coming across the border in strength. They were well supported with artillery, rockets, and mortars. Their troops were courageous, heavily armed, and well led. Brand new uniforms. Shiny weapons. Short haircuts. Incredible camouflage. They were building jungle roads of corduroy logs as they advanced. They dug deep bunkers every 20 meters along the roads which had clever overhead woven-net camouflage, underground hospitals and assembly areas for battalion-sized units. Well-hidden anti-aircraft guns protected their advance.

In the following six months, the 1st Cavalry was in the fight of its life. We had incredible helicopter air mobility and supply and medevac. Powerful artillery backed up our ground units. The Air Force fighter bombers and our Army attack helicopters were airborne hammers that would come to our support rapidly. But, in the end, it was the fighting ability of our Cav troopers with light infantry weapons that directly engaged these NVA logistics and infantry units. It was a brutal and bloody business.

By 1968 the War was in its fourth year of heavy fighting. A half million US troops and Allies were in country. The casualty lists were terrible and growing steadily ... eventually we would lose 58,000 US killed and 303,000 wounded. America had turned against the War with the final rejection following the TET 68 NVA Offensive.

When I took command of B Company in the field it was a collection of teenage soldiers with "Instant NCO" leadership that had been promoted in the field. B Company, like other infantry combat units, was nearly 100% draftees---even though only around 25% of the US forces in-country were draftees. Our company-level Lieutenants were, in general, draftees who had been hustled through OCS at Ft. Benning. The soldiers were physically strong, courageous, showed great initiative and would lay down their lives for each other. They were also incredibly resilient under enormous physical and mental pressure. They would follow orders if they made sense and they trusted the leaders over them. They were actually fun to be around and had a great sense of humor in a terrible environment. They were actually superb combat soldiers.

By this point in the war in 1968 we had nearly broken the professional career infantry NCO Corps. The older senior infantry Sergeants were by now on their second or third combat tour. The career infantry NCO Corps had suffered huge casualties. Life in a combat rifle company was also a young person's business. If you were much past 35 years old, you could not handle this life. We lived like wild animals. We carried battle loads of 90 plus pounds. We dug like moles every night to stay alive. In any given hour, we knew we could be wrenched suddenly from back-breaking boredom and physical misery to violent combat. By 1968, the senior infantry NCO's tended to fade into the Forward Operating Base (FOB) background on administrative duties. The 1st Sergeant of B Company when I first arrived and took command was a good soldier-- but essentially he ran our log pad in the rear.

Then came 1st Sgt. Emerson Trainer. What an immediate change. In the eyes of my soldiers, I was an old man at age 25. Emerson was 36 years old and a wounded veteran of the Korean War where he had served with the same B Company 2-7th Cav. He was powerfully built. He gave a sense of being the "father" of these young soldiers. Absolutely fearless. Quiet. Dignified. A teacher. Very gentle way of dealing with people. He was a natural leader. He expected to be obeyed.

Emerson could be extremely funny for effect. He would crawl into a rubber BODY BAG to sleep when it rained . . . which thrilled and grossed-out our young soldiers. Frequently, he would be armed only with a 45 caliber pistol and a TWO HEADED ENGINEER AX in the field. He was an absolute master of his trade. When we moved in the field I would rarely see him. He would seek out and walk with a squad in our 120 soldier combat company. Observer. Coach. Fearless Dad.

I admired him and trusted him. I considered him to be the co-commander of the company. He was a rock. The soldiers loved him. He was one of them. This book is his story. You can understand our admiration for 1st Sgt. Emerson Trainer when seen through the eyes of his soldiers in this book.

For nearly 50 years our B Company soldiers have stayed together. Every summer there is a reunion at a lake. Every two years there is a reunion at the Vietnam memorial. These young soldiers of ours were such good men in combat. Unsurprisingly… they still are. They take care of each other. Their families love them. They are good dads and husbands. Most have been very successful at life. They run welding shops and farms and small business. They work in health care and antique stores. A few are hugely successful financially. Many, of course, were terribly physically damaged by the war. Some suffered lasting less visible wounds. One died in prison.

But, still to this day, they love and look out for each other. They still remember how 1st Sgt. Emerson Trainer helped keep them alive because he knew what he was doing… and he cared deeply for them. He also had the credibility in their eyes gained from his earlier service as an infantry private in brutal combat.

The 1st Sergeant's son, Tim Trainer, who grew up as an Army Brat has always been part of our B Company reunions. Tim is now an extremely successful international lawyer and published author. He also had served at a later time as an Army enlisted soldier. Tim loves his dad… this great man who we called "Top."

This book, Fortunate Son, that Tim has pulled together about his father is a gift to all of us. Tim . . . you are one of us.

Barry McCaffrey, General

US Army, Retired

August 28, 2016

INTRODUCTION

What Did You Do in the War, Daddy? was the title of a mid-1960s comedic movie that was set in World War II. The antics in the movie may well be a veil. Who really wants to delve into the reality and horrors of war? Does anyone really want to know what the men who fight experience? The question posed by the film's title is one that many military brats, including myself, may be hesitant or afraid to ask. For me and other military brats, I suspect, questions linger when a parent leaves home for a tour of duty (deployment) in a war zone.

We know they leave for a war zone. Intellectually, we know it will be a dangerous place and that bad things could happen and, in fact, will happen. But still, a huge information void exists—what are our parents doing, what are they feeling, and do they really need to be there.

During the 1960s, when I was living through my father's two tours of duty in Vietnam, the evening news, in graphic fashion, brought some of the sights and sounds of war into the American home. Those reports, however, didn't really answer the question—what was my father doing? When my father returned home, he volunteered small bits and pieces over the years, but not much.

In the late 1990s, my father flew to Washington, D.C., for a reunion. He stayed at my house because I lived in a D.C. suburb. I drove him to the hotel where the reunion was taking place. My plan was to drop him off and return home. But, when I drove up in front of the hotel entrance, there was something in his voice when he asked me to go in and meet these men he had served with years earlier. I did not feel like I could say no, but I didn't want to go. Logically, I knew that these men had faced horrible things and I didn't want, or need, to hear about them. While that initial reunion was even worse than I imagined it might be, it started me down the path to meeting the men who served with my father during his second tour of duty in Vietnam that began late in 1968. As their first sergeant, they called my father "Top." Because he was family to them, they accepted me into their family.

Over the years, these aging Vietnam veterans have shared their stories. Most of these men, the grunts of B2-7, were still in, or barely out of, their teens when they first met my father. Through them, I've learned things about my father that I never knew. These men, whom I look upon almost as older brothers, have made this project possible. I've learned that my father's story is indelibly intertwined with their story.

Resistant, reluctant and a bit fearful describes my reaction to the initial prodding to pursue this work. For years, I resisted the men's subtle nudging and prodding because there was no material, but that was an excuse. The material existed, but not in written form. The material from various perspectives was abundant through the oral "history" as told to me by former soldiers who served with my father. The reluctance and fear existed because my father had worked a lifetime to be anonymous, never accepting of or seeking out any attention to himself. However, his efforts have been thwarted at times because of others who have felt the need to recognize his contributions to keep young men safe and alive in the worst of situations.

Perhaps the greatest prodding came from someone who had been out of my mind for nearly four decades. Our family moved a lot because the Army moves their personnel around from one posting to another. There came a point when I stopped counting all the moves—though the number of residences we had was into the teens by the time my father retired from the Army. Simply put, there are more moves than is normal for any child or family. It is a nomadic experience. One of these many moves was after my father's first tour of duty in Vietnam (this was before the use of "deployments"). In August 1967, our family of five, at the time, packed up our belongings, piled into a Mercury Comet, a small car, and drove from a small town in northeast Ohio to Ft. Ord, California.

My father took up his duties as the first sergeant of a basic training company at Ft. Ord. We moved into our family quarters, a single-family dwelling, on post shortly before the school year began in 1967.

Basic training is usually about an eight-week cycle to run new recruits, trainees as they may be called, through their initiation into the ways of the Army. Sometime during our time at Ft. Ord, a young drill instructor, Sgt. Fred Hall, became one of the "DIs" running a platoon of recruits in my father's company. At the time, I was in junior high school and, occasionally, would see Sgt. Hall at our house when my father hosted end-of-cycle parties (at the end of an eight-week cycle of basic training).

Whether it was Sgt. Hall or any of the other DIs, seeing any of them came to an abrupt halt in the fall of 1968 as we moved, yet, again. The war in Vietnam intruded again. The Army's needs for the war meant moving the family off post to another new location, new school, new faces and all the other things that come with relocation. For my father and the family, it would be another year-long tour of duty in Vietnam. Once a move occurs, whether it is classmates or DIs, everyone is part of the past, and there is no expectation of crossing paths in the future.

My father retired from the Army in early 1971. For nearly a year and a half, the Army was not part of my life. But, in July 1972, I joined the Army and began my own three years of active duty, all of it stateside. On a hot July morning in 1975, I got my final discharge papers, got into my car, drove to the Ft. Bragg commissary parking lot, stripped off my uniform and changed into civilian clothes in my car, and put the Army in the rear-view mirror for good, hoping that all those years would be buried with the intent of never being revisited.

By 2006, my father had been reuniting regularly with some of the former soldiers from his second tour of duty in Vietnam when he was in B2-7. Despite my reluctance, I had met more of the men of B2-7 after that initial introduction in the late 1990s.

The 2006 reunion in Alexandria, Virginia, which was close to my home in Maryland, was different. Before traveling to Alexandria for his reunion in November 2006, my father mentioned that Sgt. Fred Hall, retired from the Palatine, Illinois Park District, would be at the reunion. Sgt. Hall had fulfilled his military obligation and got out of the Army without having to endure a tour in Vietnam, although many of the recruits he trained did end up in Southeast Asia.

It had been thirty-eight years since Fred Hall, a young, very fit and trim DI had made any appearance in my life. Since 2006, however, Fred and I have become regular attendees at reunions of men who served with my father in B2-7. In addition to the reunions in Washington, D.C., we have both become regular attendees at Jerry Gast's annual summer gathering of men who served with my father. Although neither Sgt. Hall nor I served in Vietnam, we are bound together because of my father. Over time, Sgt. Hall, Fred, began to nudge me, prod me to write something about my father. At reunions, whether in Washington or at Gast's lakeside cabin, the stories or references of my father came up frequently.

Every summer, at a lakeside cabin, where perhaps ten, a dozen or more B2-7 Vietnam veterans would reunite, they retell old jokes, insult each other as if they are still 20 years old, and remember. Over the years, some of their recollections, outside of earshot of my father, were directed at me about my father. As the years have passed and Fred Hall's prodding and encouragement continued, it became clear that the time had arrived for this to be undertaken. More importantly, those who served with my father in Vietnam agreed to provide material, making this a possibility. Once the subject was raised, it became clear that they wanted to contribute and they did so very openly.

Ultimately, this work is not about just one soldier. Instead, it is about how a number of men, most barely out of their teens, somehow found themselves in the Army, in Vietnam and in the fog of a war zone. They served, exhibited extreme courage, fought for one another, came home, raised families, and realized that the short time they spent together in their youth under the worst of conditions was a bond that could not be thrust aside and forgotten.

This is a work that attempts to recognize the contributions of all of these men. No one person is truly responsible for their survival. They survived their ordeals because they were willing to die for one another. They were dedicated to keeping each other alive night and day. And, despite the short time they may have spent with each other, the bonds forged in that crucible remain strong to this day. As one summed it up, "I hated the Army but would do anything for the guys."

There was no intent to set out to answer the question "What did you do in the war, daddy?". Nevertheless, over a number of years spending some time with those who served in B2-7 with my father, a partial answer to the question flowed forth, albeit, piecemeal. It may also fill a void for the loved ones of these men as their experiences and actions while they served are also included in the following pages and provide glimpses of what they did during the war. While the war may remain controversial, the acts and actions of these men who fought in it were heroic and they are deserving of everyone's respect.

CHAPTER 1

BEFORE THE DELUGE

T he ground shook and reverberated through the skeletal frames of the housing. It felt like tremors from an earthquake. We seemed to be sitting above ground zero or near it. But, there was no earthquake, and to the extent there was a ground zero, it was miles away. It was the routine impact of tank shells off in the distance. Sometimes the sudden impact of shells were seconds apart and other times minutes.

This wasn't Vietnam, it was Ft. Knox, Kentucky. Housing units on post shook and shuddered on their foundations. The fact that the structures on post remained intact was a testament to those who constructed and built the barracks, the dependent housing and the other structures at Ft. Knox. The barrage continued night and day.

Ft. Knox, where they keep all that gold, was the Army's home of armor in the 1960s. Tanks clanked along and spewed black diesel fumes into the air. It is a sprawling Army post because it needed a lot of land for tanks to fire away at targets. Also, space was needed to provide for recruits in basic training and all that comes with that—miles of backroads for marching, tank, rifle and grenade ranges, and the gas chamber. Along with all the training spaces, there have to be places for all the billeting of soldiers and their equipment.

Army posts can be and are a world unto themselves. Ft. Knox was my home from the summer of 1963 until about April 1966. There was on-post housing in named areas such as "Dietz Acres" where we lived along with hundreds of other Army families. It was possible for an Army brat to be born, attend school and graduate from high school on post. The post accommodated the needs of Army brats (accommodating the boys more than the girls) with little league baseball, a tackle football league once a kid hit ten years of age (the "Little Tankers" of course), and a teen club for the high school kids.

Ft. Knox had multiple housing areas for enlisted ranks and officers. Dietz Acres was a family housing area for enlisted men (non-commissioned officers, NCOs). Not just anyone can get family housing on post. There were requirements related to rank, and rank determined what type of family housing was available. But, rank, race, and ethnicity were irrelevant once you stepped within the walls of the schools on post. All the kids were simply Army brats. And, though there were the usual small-time mischievous things that kids can get into, they rarely did anything outlandish, perhaps because people knew how to find your dad. Discipline rolled down hill if there were problems at school.

We occupied a two-story end unit of eight units in one building. Our eight-unit building faced another eight-unit building separated only by parking for these sixteen units. Summers were loud outside because there were over fifty kids living in these sixteen units and very few were junior high or high school age. The military was integrated, and as a result, we were not aware of the level of diversity that existed. This meant many of us were the product of mixed marriages, but for most of us, this was the norm.

Because this was the early and mid-1960s, the number of mothers from foreign countries, European and Asian, and the number of households that had a parent whose native language was not English was high. This was the post-WWII generation when thousands of GIs were stationed abroad and married women from the countries where they had served. It meant that these foreign-born women came to the United States as adults, having finished their education in their home countries. Many of the wives had limited English reading and writing abilities, leaving the kids to fill some of that void. Such was our family.

Being in an intact family environment at Ft. Knox meant staying at the same school for a couple of school years, seeing kids from the previous school year. This lent normalcy and stability to dependent Army life, to the extent there are such things as normalcy and stability. Playing against the same kids in baseball and football for two years was a new and welcome experience.

Once Army brats reach a certain age, some things become so normal that they do not mentally register: the sound of distant weapons fire, the line of tanks off in the distance, visible from a school window, the cadence of troops being marched to who knows where. In some ways, it was like living in a foreign country that had restricted borders and required documents to cross into the civilian world. It felt that way only because Army brats who were not old enough to drive were dependent upon their parents or others to get them off post. The reality was that all the basic necessities were available on post and there was little reason to go into the civilian community. In the 60s, Ft. Knox was an open post as people could drive onto and off of the installation without being stopped.

Army posts are busy places. There are recruits to train all the time, even during peace time. Training, in general, has to be conducted. Proficiency levels with weapons need to be maintained. Soldiering must continue and it does. For military brats, basically, it was that our fathers (much more the case in the 1960s than today because of the larger percentage of women in today's military) had a different job than most. Although, living on post did not give me this perspective because all the dads are in the Army and wear the same work clothes. This environment can make the civilian world seem a bit strange . . . living in the same place all the time, attending only one elementary school or just one high school and never living in other parts of the world or country. Civilian life can seem boring.

Slightly more than a year into the comfortable life of Ft. Knox, news of the Tonkin Gulf incident aired, but little or no notice was taken by us Army brats or so it was within my circle of friends. Maybe we were too young to take note of how something that far away could have such an impact on us.

There were indications of change, but at a certain age the indicators can be missed. We were used to the sound of tanks firing off in the distance and the regular rattling of our housing units, but the ear-piercing sound of a jet streaking over the housing area caused heads to snap upward. Watching it streaking toward the tank range, the pilot fired off the jet's ordnance. This added dimension to the training was one sign of change. Indications of change were about to increase.

Slowly, but regularly, the sight of large moving vans became the norm. It was easier to notice their appearance in front of someone's housing unit in the summer when school was out. Family belongings had to be packed up. But, the sight of moving vans was not limited to the summer. The Army is not on a school-year calendar schedule.

The sight of moving vans also meant that classmates began moving out. There was no formality or recognition to the loss of classmates because of a move. Classmates simply left with barely any mention other than to say, "We're moving." Friends and classmates, here one day and gone the next. At the ripe age of eleven or twelve, we did not have discussions about our moves or our futures. We did not ask questions of our departing classmates. Frequent moves were just part of Army life. In fact, by the time Army brats were old enough to start school, it was not uncommon to find that they had several moves under their belts.

It is as if the Army knows when people are getting too comfortable and a change of environment and scenery are necessary. Ft. Knox, of all places, is where there were friends, the same school and familiarity for a few short years. Subconsciously, I knew that the day would come when it is time to pack up and move. When it happens, it really is no surprise. At some point, it has to be expected.

My father must have tired of Ft. Knox. At some point, there was talk of putting in for a transfer to another post somewhere in the continental U.S. But, time passed and nothing happened. There were pick-up baseball games in the summer with kids in the housing area who had become familiar faces and friends. My friends and I wandered around in familiar woods in our housing area during the summer, and I played for the same football coaches for more than one football season.

Eventually, however, orders came down, and it was our turn to pack up and move out. It was Spring 1966. The Army had moving down to a science or so it seemed. Once the process began, it took little time. We were not moving to another post in the continental U.S. Instead, it was a move back to the civilian world, my father's home state of Ohio. He would go off to Ft. Bragg, without the family, for a couple of months of jungle training before his first year-long tour of duty in Vietnam.

With the jungle training at Ft. Bragg behind him, my father boarded a train on a misty August morning in 1966 for his cross-country trek to California. From there, he flew to Vietnam.

This was the beginning of the nearly annual changes. It was the beginning of the deluge of new faces and places about every twelve to sixteen months. This was the beginning of digesting the reality of war. The network news transmitted the images of what the Vietnam War looked like—every night in living color, if you had a color television. The coverage was graphic. It had the sounds to go along with the visuals of what war looked like. This was different than watching a World War II movie with John Wayne or any other actors or a documentary of WWII.

For the '60s generation, it was the ultimate reality television before "reality television" became a way of marketing new programs. Watching the war every night, realizing its gruesomeness, cruelty and inhumanity, the war found its way into the subconscious.

In addition to the news, there were black and white photographs. My father took pictures and sent some home. They depicted reality as well. The pictures eliminated the need to ask if where he was and whether what he was doing was dangerous. The pictures answered those questions. He was living what I was seeing in still photos. To the question, why was I looking at them? My mother was one of those post-war foreign wives/mother. Her English reading and writing skills were extremely limited and the job of writing every letter to my father and reading every one that arrived was mine. I opened and read every letter that arrived. That was one of my responsibilities.

In the most unpredictable way, the mind can play its games during the night when you're asleep. It happened to me once. Before leaving for school, I had a moment of panic, looking in kitchen drawers, on the table, under anything on the kitchen counter. I was convinced that the Department of the Army had sent a notification. Whatever my mind was working on during sleep, it had flooded into consciousness in the early morning. The half minute or minute of panic subsided. There was nothing.

Living in a civilian community meant mentally compartmentalizing. School mates continued with their lives as if all is fine and nothing unusual is happening to them or around them, unless an older sibling or cousin or other relative was drafted. It meant going about daily routines as if there was nothing different about me compared to any of the other kids. In some ways, it was about playing along with "normal." Watching the war at night, the sounds of it, the war was a private matter. There was no reason to talk about Vietnam with anyone.

The first tour of duty in Vietnam created the template for how to manage the balance of keeping things as normal as possible . . . school, home life, and the war. It was not as if civilian kids did anything that was different from military brats. It was that our dads had very different types of jobs. Their dads generally came home from work every day. Our dads were gone for a solid year and where they went came with some high risks. It was not good to dwell on the possibilities of a tour of duty that was short of a full year.

That phrase, "No news is good news," was taken to heart. There was so much truth in it. Although I would never step foot in Vietnam during the war years, it would impose itself on me, my family, and tens of thousands of other military families. And, for thousands of teenage boys, young men, it would be the end of the innocence.

CHAPTER 2

YOU'RE IN THE ARMY NOW

T he recruits entered the army from every corner of the country and from varied socio-economic backgrounds. A basic training platoon would include college graduates and high school dropouts, straight-laced kids as well as those with juvenile or criminal records. There reached a point when being in college did not guarantee an exemption from the draft.

During Vietnam, there came a time when the Army needed bodies, and it mattered little whether a recruit was physically fit or not. The Army would work to whip bodies into some level of fitness sufficient to fight a war. A recruit that arrived forty or fifty pounds overweight was bound to lose most of it during basic training, guaranteed if basic training was during the summer months.

Strange things can and do happen during the initial phases of anyone's term of active duty. The arrival at the Army's "reception" station is neither hugs and kisses nor a warm and fuzzy welcome, but the first hint of things to come. Arriving at the reception station, none of the drill instructors care whether a recruit is a draftee or a volunteer.

The first several days at the "reception station" are about getting things in order so that when basic training actually begins, time is not wasted on things like obtaining boots, uniforms, and other basic necessities. The trend of longer hair in the '60s allowed a recruit's hairstyle to be a part of his identity, a distinct way of identifying someone during those first few days, but something happens after everyone gets a haircut . . . the same haircut. Suddenly, it is nearly impossible to recognize guys until there is a renewed familiarity with the way guys look in their new Army look—buzz cut and olive green.

Everybody is "shorn like a sheep," thought Chris Sayre. Sayre remembers that after the hair was shorn, drill sergeants had a generic nickname for all recruits.

"They called all of us 'dickheads'."

During basic training, it is possible for a platoon to be called out and ordered into formation at any time. It was not unusual for a DI to march into the barracks screaming for his trainees to get into formation and for a whole platoon of trainees to be standing at attention wearing nothing but skivvies or less, just a towel wrapped around the waist. Anyone who has served in the military and watched television episodes of M*A*S*H understands the reality and hilarity of the things that can and do happen.

Basic training is the first Army (military) experience that everyone will have in common. Long exhausting days were followed by nights of interrupted sleep. Every second or third night, trainees had to pull an hour as the fireguard in the barracks. It was a long hour. If it wasn't fireguard duty, it might be an hour spent walking around in the middle of the night, pacing repeatedly around the mess hall and orderly room, a small building where the company commander, executive officer, and the first sergeant had their offices.

Trainees learned, one way or another, the difference between their left and their right. Trainees found out that DIs have a strange or sick sense of humor. DIs may pop CS gas canisters, commonly referred to as tear gas, before a DI has fully explained how to get a snug fit for the gas masks, resulting in trainees choking on the gas, scattering in all directions because they haven't been able to get their masks on properly.

DIs seemed to enjoy watching some trainees collide into trees during a strange relay competition. It was the kind of relay race that no one had seen before the Army and, probably, never after the Army. Each platoon lined up. A man would run down to where a DI was holding a baseball bat and the trainee would put a forehead on the knob of the bat and make ten revolutions around the knob while the DI counted. The trainee's attempt to run back to his platoon so the next man up could run down to the bat was hilarious. The problem was that dizziness ensued after those ten revolutions, causing some to veer off-course and into impediments, including trees.

There is also that other, more serious aspect to basic training. The trainees who enter the Army with little or no experience with weapons and the tools of warfare will be introduced to some of them. They learned to tear down and put their individual weapon back together under timed conditions. They came to appreciate the raw power of an M-60 machine gun. They were surprised by the distance that grenade fragments can travel. And, their attention was captured by the explosion of a claymore mine when it was time to learn how to set it.

The path to the Army and basic training, however, is unique and a distinct journey for each person and can come with unexpected surprises. The group of men who ended up crossing paths with Top started their journey from different places and in different ways.

Dale Beierman

Dale Beierman grew up on a farm in Minnesota. He came from a very small town of about a thousand residents. It was a homogenous place where almost everyone was of the same religion. Like many of his generation, he was the son of a World War II veteran. His father had served and fought in North Africa and Italy. A sense of service tended to be instilled by the WWII generation.

Dale recalls, "I checked out the Vietnam War, thought I really knew what was going on. I was a proponent of it."

In August 1967, at the age of eighteen, he volunteered for the draft. He was sent to Ft. Campbell, Kentucky, for basic training.

To say the Army was different from Beierman's hometown surroundings might be an understatement.

"I was in total shock the first three weeks," he recalls. He had been active while in school and had traveled around a little, but it was very limited. "I never interacted with black people, Hispanic people. I'd never rubbed shoulders with them or anything so it was a pretty big adjustment." It was not simply being around the kind of people he had never interacted with, but also being away from home. "The harsh reality, you were by yourself. You're all alone. I came from a large family. All of a sudden, I was alone. That was the biggest adjustment."

Jesse ("Pops") Groves

Jesse ("Pops") Groves was drafted and entered the Army in October 1967. The Army was a very different experience from what he was used to growing up in Illinois and helping out on a farm. He was sent to Ft. Bliss, Texas, for basic training. His nickname, Pops, was given to him because of his "advanced" age upon being drafted at 22 years old, a few years older than most of those sharing in the experience.

Those few years in age made a difference. He had worked and knew hard work. He also took his working responsibilities seriously enough so that he knew what had to be done without the need of constant oversight.

DIs changed Pops' view of the world in some ways.

"I was used to a pretty simple life. When people told you they were going to do something, they were going to do it. Your handshake was your bond. That's the way it was. I got in the Army and found out that that's not the way it was. People weren't honest with you. They would trick you into doing stuff that if they were honest, you wouldn't have done."

He learned more about human nature from his exposure to DIs and others during basic training.

Pops' farm work and general work background prepared him well to deal with the physical rigors of basic training. He liked the simulated hand-to-hand combat fighting using pugil sticks, the pole with padding on each end.

"They'd put you in the middle. What they'd do is put me in the middle and there'd be one guy facing me and then they'd have a whole bunch of guys behind me and knock me over. That didn't bother me, scare me. I liked that. I did like that where you could knock somebody in the head with that stick. But, the DI would send guys back at me. I guess I was doing too good a job so they'd send other guys back while I'm fending off one guy."

Pops' basic training challenges were dealing with the mental aspects of being in the Army. The overall regimen of the Army was a challenge.

"The perfect soldier is someone who doesn't think at all. A robot would be a perfect soldier. The problem I had is that I was used to being a civilian where you thought a little bit. They didn't want me thinking. Every time I thought, I got in trouble. It took me a while to understand where this train was going. I was one of their pet examples. That's not the way you do it. You do it the other way. But after a while, I sort of, I got with the program. I said, well, this is the way it's gotta be. This is where I am, so this is what I've gotta do."

Once there was acceptance of the situation, things got better.

"The mental part of it, I had to get the idea of civilian out of my head before I could focus on the military side of it. And that's the way it was. But, once that happened . . . "

With that, Pops went on with fulfilling his obligations.

Gerald "Jerry" Gast

Jerry Gast was a nineteen-year old draftee in August 1967 and headed to Ft. Leonard Wood, Missouri, for basic training.

Jon "Snag" Johnson

Jon Johnson was also only nineteen years old when he "volunteered" for the draft, entering the Army in January 1968 and being sent to Ft. Campbell, Kentucky.

Rich Dorsey

At twenty-one years old, Rich Dorsey was a couple of years older than most when he got drafted and entered the Army in February 1968. Dorsey had gotten deferments because of college. College, however, was not his thing at that point in his life.

"I played around with college and all that and that's why I didn't get drafted till later. I was too immature at the time. I couldn't see any purpose for it. I kept flunking out and, finally, got a job at the Y as a lifeguard and that's when the draft notice came after I lost my deferment. They sent me to Ft. Campbell, Kentucky, but they had so many called up at that time that they sent me to Ft. Bliss, Texas, for basic."

Dorsey understood what the Army was trying to do to recruits.

"What they try to do is totally break you so they can remold you. Frankly, I needed to be broken. When I went into the service, it was pandemonium, it was confusion, it was not knowing up from down and, of course, when they shave your head, run you through the lines of all the shots, move you from place to place on cattle trucks and all that, you were broken and I needed to be broken."

After completing basic training, Dorsey headed to Ft. Polk, Louisiana, for AIT.

Jack Jeter

Jack Jeter, a Texan, was one of the older guys of this group. He was twenty-three years old and married when his number came up. He was inducted in May 1968 and did his basic training at Ft. Polk, Louisiana.

Chris Sayre

Unlike Jeter, Chris Sayre was still single a year out of high school and was a nineteen-year old draftee going to basic training at Ft. Dix, New Jersey, in June 1968. Simply receiving the draft notice in 1968 made him think he was a dead man. Like others, Sayre went to infantry AIT at Ft. Polk, Louisiana.

"As soon as you knew you were going to AIT in Ft. Polk, you knew you were screwed."

He realized that Vietnam was in his future.

But, while at Ft. Polk, he learned that the Army does care about the personal health and hygiene of its soldiers before sending them to Vietnam.

"I always had bad teeth as a kid growing up," Sayre explains. "I had a calcium deficiency as a kid. I know that when I went to AIT, I went to a dentist. They said they didn't have time to fix my teeth so the dentist says, 'Oh my god, we need to pull your teeth'. He says, 'You'll never survive with the teeth you have'.

"So one day, they pulled a lot of teeth and gave me a full upper denture. I went back to the barracks, and I was laying in the bunk in pain and agony. All of a sudden, a cattle truck pulls up, and I hear the drill sergeant ask, 'Where's that fucking Sayre?' and someone said, 'He's up in his bunk,' and the Drill sergeant tells somebody to come up and tell me to get my ass down here. So, this kid comes running up the stairs and says, 'Hey, the drill sergeant wants you down there'.

"I was not in the mood and told the kid to go down and tell him that I just had a bunch of teeth pulled. I ain't coming down. Unfortunately for me, the kid was too scared of the drill sergeant to deliver my message. So, I crawl my ass out of bed, and I go down the stairs and as soon as the Drill Sergeant sees me he says, 'Get down and give me 50'. So, I'm down there doing these fucking pushups, and he's dismissing the rest of the company when he comes over and says, 'Where the fuck have you been, boy?'

"I said 'I just had a bunch of teeth pulled Drill Sergeant' and he pulls me up off the ground and hugged me and said, 'Oh, I'm really sorry.' From that point on he was my best friend."

The Army had relieved Sayre of one concern, his dental needs.

Fred Hall

Fred Hall wanted to serve, but not the way it turned out. He wanted to be a Navy pilot. As a college senior in Massachusetts and before signing on the dotted line, he took tests, something a college student is good at, and scored well enough to go to Officer Candidate School (OCS). The scores were impressive enough to get a verbal promise of flight school in his future (ahh, yes, a verbal promise . . . a life lesson).

A surprise awaited him when he went for his physical examination. As a college senior, he was not aware of one vision-related condition that might pose a problem. He learned that he was colorblind, dashing his hopes of becoming a pilot.

Fred Hall, however, was undeterred in his desire to serve. He pursued the possibility of enlisting in the Marine Corps and going to OCS for the Marine Corps with the plan to try to get onto the underwater demolition team. He liked the water and given his past experience as a lifeguard, he wanted to work toward qualifying for the underwater demolition team. Although his Navy test results were acceptable to the Marine Corps, he needed to undergo another physical examination. Once again, the physical examination uncovered a problem—a pinprick in his ear. The ear problem would prevent him from going deep underwater. His pursuit of serving in the military seemed to be at an end.

Having exhausted his plans to serve, he finished college in Massachusetts and headed to Illinois for graduate school. He also got married. He had a job in northern Illinois. Fred Hall seemed somewhat settled by August 1965.

The Army, however, came calling a year later. He was twenty-four years old, married and his wife was teaching. His situation was a bit more complicated than for younger draftees. In order to delay his entry into the Army, he "enlisted" as a reluctant volunteer for a two-year active duty commitment but was able to work out a delayed entry in order to deal with moving his wife back to New England. After having concluded that the military was not to be, Fred Hall entered the Army in January 1967 and found himself in basic training at Ft. Dix, New Jersey.

In Fred Hall's case, it may have been his advanced "age" entering the Army, his more disciplined experiences before the Army and his increased sense of responsibility because he was married that contributed to his high level of performance in basic training and subsequent graduation from AIT at Ft. Ord, California. By June, 1967, he was finished with his initial training programs but was in limbo because of his application for a direct commission to be an officer. Hall was held over with his AIT company because of his application for a direct commission. He was advised to drop his request for Officer Candidate School in light of his direct commission application. He was now killing time awaiting the Army's decision. He did, however, get promoted to Private First Class. While waiting, he spent time with special services, which meant assisting in managing sports activities.

Time dragged on while waiting for the Army's answer about a direct commission, and eventually, Hall became permanent party to the company that he had trained with in AIT. He was made an acting Corporal and an assistant drill instructor. A major benefit of being an acting Corporal was access to the NCO Club where he was able to socialize and meet other NCOs.

The Department of the Army turned down Hall's request for a direct commission. The only written reason he recalls seeing for the rejection was that he had failed to exhibit sufficient desire to be an Army officer as evidenced by his withdrawal of his request for Officer Candidate School, which he had done on the advice of a Lieutenant Colonel.

As so many have learned, the Army works in strange ways and trying to figure it out is futile.

William (Bill) Montgomery

In 1966, Bill Montgomery was a naïve twenty-year old young man. He was not at all familiar with the ways of the Army or the military generally.

"I got drafted when I was twenty. I went down to the induction center in Houston and they told me I had passed the tests for OCS. Back then you didn't have to have college, you just have to pass tests and be reviewed by a panel of field grade officers [major, lieutenant colonel and colonel] and they would let you go to OCS. They asked if I wanted to go to Officer Candidate School and asked what I get if I do that. They said that I'd have to sign up, enlist for three years instead of being drafted for two, and then they told me about the benefits. It sounded good so I said sign me up."

Montgomery signed up for three years and was inducted.

"Then I got to the reception station at Ft. Polk and took some tests, and the sergeant called me over, told me I did good on my tests and said do you want to take the test for OCS. I said I already did. He said, 'No, you didn't. You can't take that test until you come here and pass the tests you just did.' I said, 'So they scammed me in Houston'."

Montgomery was referring to the fact that he'd been influenced in signing up for three years before being inducted.

The sergeant did not seem to believe that Montgomery had been scammed at the induction center in Houston. Montgomery asked the sergeant at the reception station if his term of service would revert back to a two-year obligation if he did not get into OCS. He thought the sergeant would die laughing at the question. He had signed up for a three-year term of service. He was off to Ft. Polk, Louisiana, for basic training.

Edward (Edd) Holtz

Edd was a year out of high school with a menial job of loading furniture. One morning in the summer of 1967 when the alarm woke him, he did not feel like getting up and going to work. And, he did not want to make up some excuse for missing work. He had no plans for college, no girlfriend and, frankly, no obligations, but he also realized that he would eventually be drafted and probably headed to Vietnam. Thinking like a rational nineteen-year old, he thought if he died tomorrow, his parents would be upset for a while, maybe six months or so, and then they probably wouldn't care anymore because they would think he was in heaven and all would be okay.

An hour and a half after waking, he finally got up and dressed. He concluded that he might as well join up and get the military obligation done. Rather than wait for the draft notice that he believed would come, he volunteered for the draft. A few weeks later and a month after his 19th birthday, Edd Holtz joined the Army on September 14, 1967, and headed for Ft. Leonard Wood, Missouri, for basic training.

"Your first five days at the reception station you play a lot of cards. I had a deck. They picked us up at reception, marched us to the basic training supply depot, and stood us on an asphalt parking lot. You could see vapor coming up off of the asphalt, and we're all standing there. I think it was 'at ease', but it would have been like a 'parade rest' at ease. We're still in a position. You were supposed to run over to the stairs, run up onto the loading dock, run down to your unit, get your bedding and get back into formation.

"When I came out of the depot with my stuff, I ran into the fucking platoon leader. He ripped me a new asshole and then turned me over to a DI who was about six feet three or four and weighed maybe 230. I'd be willing to bet, I sold clothes, that he'd take about a 48-inch jacket and about a 32 or 33-inch waist pant with a bubble butt. His fucking arms were bigger than my legs. He had a tooth connected to a bridge in his mouth and he'd suck on the damn thing and push it back and forth in his mouth as he stared through your eyes to the back of your head. He made guys cry. And, they gave me to this DI.

"So they've got me on the asphalt. I'm doing push-ups until I can't do anymore push-ups. And, he finally put his boot on my butt and then let the weight of his leg take me down. I couldn't stay up. So he rolled my ass over and had me doing sit-ups until I couldn't do anymore sit-ups. And then, he had me roll over again and get into a front leaning rest position so that my hands are burning on the asphalt and guys next to me would get into the front leaning position and out of the front leaning rest position and he still had me in it. He finally stood my ass up and told me to never call the Lieutenant 'Lieutenant.' I called him 'Sir' because I didn't know any better. They thought I was fucking with them both. That's what started this shit."

What transgression led to Edd's physical stress? Edd had called the Lieutenant 'Lieutenant'—a learning opportunity, if you will. Edd learned that it was more appropriate to use "Sir" when responding to this Lieutenant. The learning point was not a complete success because Edd responded "Sir" whether it was the Lieutenant or the DI, creating more opportunities for Edd's Army education to continue. DIs, being enlisted personnel, not officers, should not be addressed with "Sir."

After Edd and the other inductees were marched back to the company area with their bedding and other supplies, they were once again called out to formation by the DI. The DI wanted to know if anyone had a deck of cards and when no one admitted to having a deck of cards, the DI threatened to go through everyone's possessions and if a deck was found, things would get very uncomfortable.

When the DI asked again, a lone voice in the back of the formation, Edd, admitted to having a deck of cards. He was ordered to the front of the formation.

"And I've got this big smirk on my face because I know I'm going to go through the same thing I just went through on the parking lot. I just fucked up. Why me? Why am I the only voice that has a deck of cards? A big smirk still on my face. It sent this guy right up the wall, and he's nuts with me now. Doesn't know what to do with me. He's already made me do a thousand push-ups, already made me do a thousand sit-ups, and already had me in a front leaning rest position for three days. What is he going to do to punish me now?

"He looked over his shoulder. One whole barracks was a latrine—toilets, urinals, showers, sinks, and it leaked water from all of this shit into a puddle as long as the barracks in between two barracks. In that puddle, it looked orange and brown and green and hairy and slimy and shitty. He looked at me and told me to go over there and get down and low crawl through the puddle. I can't begin to tell you how relieved I was because this was going to be easy. I couldn't do another push-up. I crawled through to the end of it and said 'What now Sergeant' and he told me to turn around and crawl back so I turned around and crawled back.

"He said 'Get over here'. I stood up and this shit is just oozing and dripping off of me. I ran up to him and stood in front of him. He looked down at me and said 'You ever going to answer me again with a smirk on your face?' I said, 'No Sir, Sergeant.' And my smirk reappeared. I couldn't stop it. I could see in his eyes that he wanted to kick the shit out of me to set an example. He just glared at me then said, 'Get the fuck out of my sight'."

Things did get better, but Edd's general sentiment was he "didn't like platoon sergeants that were trained to try to tear us apart as civilians and put us back together as soldiers. There was a piece of me that just always seemed to go against the grain."

Paul Decker

Paul grew up in a blue-collar household with five siblings. Like practically all other similar families, money was not plentiful.

He had an itch to fly. As a high school senior in Binghamton, New York, he worked an after-school job at a local gas station and used the money earned to pay for flying lessons at the nearby county airport. Though he had been taking lessons, there wasn't enough money in the household for him to continue after high school and he never soloed.

Weeks before his high school graduation in 1968, he went to Syracuse to see an Army recruiter. Paul told the recruiter about his interest in flying, and the recruiter said the Army had a rotary wing program to fly helicopters. Paul said he would be interested in the helicopter program.

He traveled to Syracuse again to take the Warrant Officer flight test. He did extremely well, an easy test in his mind based on what he had already learned. Going over the test with the recruiter, Paul recounts what the recruiter said.

"You scored great. We can get you into the program. You've got two options. One is to go sign the contract for three years, and we guarantee you flight school in Ft. Rucker, Alabama. The other is to enlist for two years unassigned. I can verbally guarantee you that you'll get into flight school."

After considering his options, Paul enlisted just a week or two before high school graduation. He opted for the two-year unassigned option. All the while, what played in the back of his mind at the time was the likelihood that he would still get to flight school. With papers signed, Paul was on his way to basic training at Ft. Dix, New Jersey, within a week to ten days after his high school graduation.

Training and More Training

Active duty time can be consumed by training. Even as the build-up of troops in Vietnam was in high-gear moving into the latter half of the 1960s, basic training was supplemented by more training. What comes after basic training, which takes eight weeks?

Fred Hall finished both basic training and AIT. By late summer or early fall 1967, Hall knew that becoming an officer was not to be. He recalls his first sergeant saying, "Fred, you should let me set up a meeting with the old man," meaning the company commander.

Hall met with his company commander who explained the options. By this time, Hall was a Specialist 4th Class but wearing acting sergeant stripes.

The CO explained, "Here's what I see as your options. First, you can just stay here. You just wait for your orders to go to Vietnam because you are very unlikely to be put on a list for anyplace other than Vietnam. Your second option, we can still get you into OCS at Ft. Benning."

By this time, Hall was not too keen on the OCS option, telling the CO, "Sir, it'll take a while for all the paperwork to clear and then I'll probably have a brief leave, and then I'll have six months down there, and then two more years added onto that. I've already got seven or eight months in. No, I think I'm going to stay as an enlisted man, put my two years in and go home."

The CO understood Hall's thinking. The CO was not finished with the options available. He explained to Hall, "Here's your third option. You've been excellent as an assistant drill instructor. I know I can get you into Drill Sergeant school."

Hall chose option three and went to school to become a DI. He stayed at Ft. Ord, California, and attended Drill Sergeant School. Time. More training and schools kill time. He recalled that back then Drill Sergeant School ate up another couple of months. He graduated from the school as the outstanding graduate of his class, topping the class academically and second in the physical challenges of the course. Fifty years later, he is still upset that his possibly lackadaisical hand grenade throw may have cost him the top spot on the physical side of the course.

The Drill Sergeant course graduation ceremony began on a Saturday morning. That morning, the first sergeant of his AIT company handed Hall orders to sign out of his AIT training brigade that day and to sign into a basic training brigade. Essentially, these orders would assure him a year-long stabilized tour as a drill sergeant at Ft. Ord. All he had to do was to sign out of one company and sign in to another that day—that Saturday. If he stayed in the AIT training brigade, there was no assurance of a year-long stabilized tour. Hall concluded that he had till midnight to sign out and sign in to his new brigade. His loyalty to the company that had supported him stopped him from signing out before the graduation ceremony. Thus, he graduated from Drill Sergeant School while still in the AIT training brigade.

Toward the end of the graduation proceedings, Hall was going through a reception line that included his company commander and a colonel who was in charge of the AIT training brigade. The company commander lamented the fact that they were losing Hall to a basic training brigade. Hall recalls that the colonel gave him a verbal order that he was not to sign out from the colonel's command.

Hall, following the colonel's orders, did not sign out of his AIT training company. Instead, he partied on Saturday and into Sunday. On Monday morning, he had his new drill instructor hat and was all spit and polished when he arrived for duty at his AIT company, the same one where he had had a supportive company commander, who had, in the meantime, departed that company. The first sergeant who had been helpful and supportive was still there.

Having graduated as the outstanding graduate of his class, Hall recalls clearly the memorable greeting from the first sergeant. "You dumb son-of-a-bitch." Hall was confused. The first sergeant handed over a new set of orders—90th Replacement Station, Vietnam.

"What happened" was all that came out of Hall's mouth.

The first sergeant said, "No, you tell me what happened. I busted my butt to get you orders and I got them." Hall explained what the colonel had told him on Saturday at the graduation ceremony.

Finding himself in a bind, Hall decided that the only way to fix things was to talk to the colonel who had given him the verbal order. First, he had to overcome obstacles, military protocol. Lowly enlisted soldiers do not just show up and talk to any colonel. Prevented from meeting with the colonel, Hall opted to talk to the brigade sergeant major. After a brief discussion with the sergeant major, Hall simply walked out of the sergeant major's office, down the hall to the colonel's office, without an appointment, and knocked.

With proper military bearing, Hall stood before the colonel and explained what had happened and argued his case for why he should remain at Ft. Ord and train recruits. He told the colonel that he had been prepared to go to Vietnam before he had been sent to drill sergeant school, but that it seemed to make little or no sense for the Army to send him to Vietnam after the Army had just sent him to drill sergeant school. Hall had made a good case for himself. With a phone call or two, the colonel had his orders to Vietnam revoked and his orders to go to a basic training brigade reinstated.

The reinstated orders for Hall to report to a basic training brigade meant that it also assured him of a year-long stabilized tour. More importantly, it would take him to the end of his two-year tour of duty commitment.

Bill Montgomery believed that he had been scammed into signing up for three years. He was able to pick a military occupational specialty, better known as an "MOS" in case OCS did not pan out. After completing basic training at Ft. Polk, it was on to supply school. Those high scores on the tests he had taken—twice—finally, led to OCS, which lasted six months. Once he was done with OCS, he was a newly minted second lieutenant. By this time, he had burned the first year of his three-year obligation.

Montgomery recalls, "This is where I think the Army was nuts back then. They took us out of OCS and put us in as training officers in basic training companies. We didn't practice, we didn't train to be officers. It was infantry OCS and we didn't do anything infantry [in basic training]. We just taught trainees how to march, did inspections and such."

Montgomery spent the better part of his second year in the Army as a basic training officer. During that time, he met up with another young officer who had a jungle school patch on his fatigues. Montgomery decided it would be a cool patch to have so he applied to go to jungle school in Panama. For Montgomery, except for the several weeks of jungle school in Panama, he spent nearly two years stateside.

Stateside time for others was shorter. All the others, being enlisted personnel, had two things in common. All of them went from basic training then to AIT. Most went to Ft. Polk, Louisiana, for AIT.

Paul Decker, who had done well on tests for flight school, was stunned to find that the Army had given him the MOS for infantry: 11 Bravo. Worse yet, he would be headed to Vietnam as an infantryman.

"My parents contacted our congressman, and there was a big to do about, well, he was verbally guaranteed flight school. The bottom line was the government said show me in writing where we guaranteed you this school. Otherwise, you have no options."

Indeed, there was no other option.

Holtz, who had a turbulent beginning at the reception station, before ever arriving at his basic training company, spent additional time with more training after AIT. He took to soldiering. He went on to NCO school and jump school before spending a brief period of time in an AIT company running recruits. All of the training courses and the one AIT cycle of pushing recruits through training took a good amount of his first year in the Army.

Dale Beierman and Jerry Gast's routes were similar to Holtz's except that Holtz was the only one to go to jump school. Otherwise, these three went to NCO school after completing AIT. And, like Holtz, their NCO school experience led to running recruits through AIT training for one cycle, a way of earning those buck sergeant stripes.

Dorsey, Groves, Jeter, Johnson, and Sayre, like Decker, had a more direct route to Vietnam. After basic training and AIT, they were headed to Southeast Asia. But, at least for Sayre, he could go to Vietnam with a smile, though not much of one, after the Army had taken care of his teeth, knowing that it would not be his teeth that threatened his health and well-being.

CHAPTER 3

END OF THE INNOCENCE

E vents ratcheted up in 1968 with the TET Offensive and the siege of U.S. Marines at Khe Sanh. The year resulted in the highest number of U.S. military members killed during the war. The lethalness of the war was worsening and the need to feed the war machine grew. For those aged nineteen to twenty-one, that age group was hit hardest, accounting for over 32,000 killed during the war.

Soldiers arriving in Vietnam did not travel with a cohesive unit that would travel to the country, serve, fight, and survive together. The guys that made up a platoon in basic training or in AIT did not proceed together to Vietnam. Rather, they arrived and would be sent off in small groups or individually as replacements to various units all over Vietnam.

Jesse Groves, or "Pops", who had been drafted in October 1967, got his initiation into Army life in basic training at Ft. Bliss, Texas, followed by AIT at Ft. McClellan, Alabama. He had a month's leave before arriving in Vietnam on April 6, 1968, a date he can't forget. Though not remembering the details, he spent his first week in Vietnam in an orientation course about what to expect as an infantryman in Vietnam. After the first week, he was headed to his ultimate unit assignment, 2nd Platoon, B2-7.

Pops' flight to the field took him to a landing zone (LZ) manned by some members of B2-7.

"I don't know what LZ we were on at the time. I think it was Evans, but I'm not sure. I hadn't been there a couple of hours before they had incoming rounds, and there was a guy or two killed the first day I was there. That was my initiation to the war. I learned to get down pretty quick. It was an eye-opener from the start," recalling his first day in the field,

Pops recalls meeting up with other soldiers already in the company when he arrived. The company, as well as other units of the 1st Cavalry Division, had participated in the operation that broke the siege of Khe Sanh that had begun in January '68.

Pops spent most of the time with a machine gun team. Initially, he was an ammo bearer. He was happy to be a slightly bulkier guy because he didn't have to walk point.

A couple of months after Pops, Jon Johnson (Snag) arrived in Vietnam. Unlike Pops, Snag received no orientation or training upon arriving in country before being sent out to the field. He did, however, spend a couple of days on a detail burning crap, literally a "shit detail" . . . a good job, before being sent to the field and assigned to the 2nd Platoon, B2-7 in June 1968. Getting to B2-7 was not a smooth trip.

"The first time I flew on a helicopter, I was scared shitless, and we end up going to an engineers' spot where they were doing landscaping, whatever. I couldn't get to the platoon so I had to stay there overnight. Needless to say, we got mortared. Then they had quad-50s going, I had never seen any of those. It was a real indoctrination." He remembers, "I had to clean my drawers out. I was scared."

Like the others, he had an infantry MOS. Snag realized learning was going to be important, relying on the guys who had already been in country. Upon joining the company, Snag became an ammo bearer for the machine gun squad.

Rich Dorsey landed in Vietnam just after the 4th of July, 1968. There was no in-country orientation. He was flown north to join B2-7 within days of arriving. Dorsey reported to B2-7 with one other replacement and both had been in AIT together. They were assigned to the 2nd platoon. Upon arrival, either the CO or the first sergeant, one of them said, "We have two positions open. One of you is to be point man and one of you is to be a grenadier, and because the grenades were so heavy, the other guy said, 'I'll take point man' and I was relieved because I knew some of the horror stories that I read about, heard about point men. Well, it was a pain in the neck. I thought, 'OK, grenadier is something I can live with and all that'.

"The captain, I don't remember him speaking with us. I think it was probably the first sergeant. He said very few words, told us what we were assigned, told us to follow orders, they would try to keep us safe if we minded what they said. It was very brief."

As they say, little things mean a lot. In Dorsey's case, he was under the mistaken impression that an air mattress would be one of those little things.

"They gave me an air mattress, and I thought I was in heaven because I'd be comfortable. So I got to the field, up by the DMZ. I remember the first night, it was very comfortable, but the mosquitos kept me up all night. A new recruit came in to report to the company, and I talked him into giving me his mosquito net for the air mattress—I didn't care if I slept on rocks, that's what I wanted."

In the early days, Dorsey was, at times, inattentive to what was happening.

"When I was new in the field, I was in the same spot with two other guys, had to be August, when we were up north. There was a sergeant that was overseeing us. One of the other guys had more field experience, he'd been through the TET Offensive. Some mortar rounds started walking in on us. I remember a more seasoned veteran throwing each of us into a foxhole. We didn't know what we were supposed to do."

Dorsey realized that there were also practical shortcomings in the preparedness of life in the field.

"The one thing they never trained you on or told you about is how to take a crap in the field. The first time I went out, I dug a trench, tried to figure out how to sit, a lousy helicopter coming into the company came down, buzzed around me three or four times, and of course, I waved to them with my middle finger."

Dale Beierman and Jerry Gast arrived in Vietnam in August 1968. They had gone to NCO school together, although at the time they didn't know each other. Both already had about a year in the Army, having gone through basic training, AIT and NCO school. That was followed by a very brief stint in running other trainees through AIT for one cycle. Both arrived in Vietnam as buck sergeants.

Gast was not supposed to be in B2-7.

"When I came into Vietnam, I was assigned to Delta Company when I was in Bien Hoa. Then they flew us up to Camp Evans, and when I got to Camp Evans, they changed me to Bravo Company. Little did I know how lucky I was. When I came into the company, they were at what they called Wonder Beach up on the Gulf of Tonkin. They had this huge bunker complex in the sands. They had ducks that would drive around, pick you up, and take you to lunch. This complex was huge, and every once in a while, I'd go in the water or they'd take you down to the beach. You could go swimming down at the beach. I thought, Vietnam is pretty good. This isn't a bad deal at all, until I went on my first patrol.

"It was probably about two weeks before I went on my first patrol. It was just 2nd Platoon out by themselves. We were clearing, walking through wood lines. When we came out of probably the second wood line, two gunships saw us walking out and thought we were gooks and opened fire with their mini-guns. So, the first time I got shot at was friendly fire.

"We had a bunch of termite mounds that we, everybody jumped behind their own termite mound. . . . We had one guy wounded. That was my education about what the war was going to be like."

Like Gast, Beierman was also initially assigned to Delta Company.

"D Company, 2-7, was notorious for getting wiped out and that's what my orders were for. I remember coming to Vietnam, and everybody would say, 'Where you getting orders for?' I'd show it them and they'd say, 'Kiss your ass goodbye, you might as well commit suicide,' or whatever. They said stuff like that. It was kind of crazy. That didn't give me too much faith listening to this about the orders I got. Then, B Company had just gotten out of the A Shau Valley and had a lot of casualties so I got sent to 1st Platoon of B Company and met the lieutenant, the platoon leader. I was a little bit nervous, listening to the stories of these guys coming out of the A Shau Valley. They'd been through it already. They were pretty battle ready and were actually at Wonder Beach when I came in up north, by Camp Evans out on the ocean. The lieutenant told me that I'd be in charge of 1st squad. I said, 'Well, Sir, I appreciate that, but could I take two weeks or three and just observe a little bit.' He just locked me up and said, 'Sergeant, you're in charge'. The first few weeks I was a bit disgusted."

That was Beierman's reward for having gone through NCO School and arriving in Vietnam as a buck sergeant.

"I pushed through and got sent out on a GOAT [ambush] right away. I was a nineteen-year old buck sergeant, a shake and bake, and took a couple of months to get things in order."

In September 1968, Bill Montgomery, Edd Holtz, and Jack Jeter arrived in Vietnam. Jeter arrived in Vietnam just a couple of days before Larry Spaulding ("Skinny") who had been in Jeter's AIT company. Like those before them, they were individual insertions, replacements, into an operational infantry company.

Two years served, Lt. Montgomery's third year in the Army would be in Vietnam. Once he arrived at B2-7, he was assigned to the 1st Platoon.

"When I first joined the company, we worked as platoons. You go out in the field with just your platoon and wander, go from here to there, from there to here. By yourself, me and the 22 or 24 other guys that made up my platoon. . . . We probably spent about a month doing that just wandering, doing patrols by myself, nothing ever happened.

"I didn't even know that till a couple, three years ago that the lieutenant before me who was killed, he was the 1st Platoon leader, he was KIA. He had actually sat on a booby trapped bomb . . . this whole area where we were wandering around in, nobody ever told me, it was heavily booby trapped. I didn't find that out till a few years ago. That would've been handy.

"The company commander, he, as I've learned over the years, was friends with the lieutenant before me who was killed. Then, when I met him, he was withdrawn and didn't want to have much to do with anybody, or want to make friends or be friendly."

With a couple of dozen soldiers under his command, Lt. Montgomery's initial experiences were truly on the job training with more than a little luck on his side.

Edd Holtz arrived in Vietnam in mid-September 1968 as a buck sergeant. Holtz's year was beginning and overlapping with guys who had been in country for months. He was joining a company that included troops who had fought in the spring to break the Khe Sanh siege. He was hearing about what B2-7 had experienced. He learned about the relocation of the company nearer to the coast where there was a bunch of foothills. He found out about the tactics the company used. The CO broke the company up into platoons and would send out platoon-sized units to fight, but instead of enemy troops, the platoons kept tripping booby traps in the foothills.

"They just walked into this shit and all of a sudden something exploded and the next thing they knew guys were screaming. They dusted themselves off, and the CO told them to move out. They'd go through it again in an hour or maybe two hours, and in a day, they could have two or three of those explosions. The gooks were eating them alive, they were making them bleed, they were freaking them the fuck out—and there's nobody to shoot. They went through months of that.

"When I joined them, it was September, and I was with them for about a month out there. The security guards for the platoon, whoever's turn it was, could fall asleep, and nobody would beat the shit out of them like I was told they were going to do stateside if you ever fell asleep when you were on guard at night. They'd fall asleep, and nobody seemed to give a shit. They knew they were safe. They'd been through Khe Sanh, the A Shau and the Street. The guys that were left were hardcore.

"I got the luxury of damn near a month with them. In that month, I got my squad. I had about two weeks of a month to break in with a squad, what to do, how to do, where to fit, where to go, and then they moved us down to Quan Loi. We went out to LZ Billy.

"So, when I look at these guys, it's almost like when you come in, a few are fearless, no contact with reality. You can do all kinds of shit. But after you've been through a firefight or a campaign, up the highway into Khe Sanh, into the A Shau Valley, almost no matter what you've done, you are past the point of 'I'm invulnerable' and you begin the rest of your tour with my next step, with my next day, with my next minute I may not be here anymore—and either you've got no problem living with that—or it's going to fucking freak you out and make you very, very scared. You'll have to live with that for the rest of your tour."

Holtz watched, observed, and took it all in. Mentally, these things would be processed in the coming months.

B2-7 moved. It moved farther south during the autumn of 1968. Quan Loi was a fair distance northwest of Saigon, but not very far from the Cambodian border. With these three new bodies, Montgomery, Gast and Holtz, a lieutenant and two buck sergeants, respectively, they were to contribute greatly to what would become a more aggressive unit . . . even if it would be for only a limited time.

Jeter and Larry Spaulding ("Skinny") were on the fast track to get into Vietnam. Both had entered the Army in May and had been together through AIT at Ft. Polk. By the end of September 1968, they were headed to Cam Ranh Bay. Although their arrival dates were a few days apart, they would be reunited under less that proper circumstances. Jeter was originally assigned to Company C and Skinny had orders for Company B.

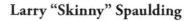

Larry "Skinny" Spaulding

Skinny explains.

"Jeter jumped off of a deuce and a half [two and a half ton truck] and I recognized him and caught up with him and asked if he'd checked in, and he said no. So, we went in to see the C Company Commander or some lieutenant and I said 'This is my cousin. Is it OK if he comes with me to Bravo Company?' Well, because Jeter hadn't checked in yet, they said go ahead."

The two of them went through the refresher course. When it was time, Jeter simply reported into B2-7 because that is where Skinny was going.

It was early October when both of them joined B2-7. They spent the rest of the month walking on patrols, but without much action.

"There was nothing going on up there. You could walk for days and see nothing but poor village people, and maybe a sniper round here or there. But, there were no firefights, not while I was there," Jeter recalls.

Chris Sayre landed in Vietnam on November 7, 1968. Like Jeter, he was on that fast track to Vietnam, having been drafted in June. When he landed in Vietnam, he disembarked the plane and saw the men headed home.

"They looked old and fatigued. They didn't look nineteen to me. They were standing on the tarmac to board the freedom bird to go home. I was thinking, 'Oh my God, look at these guys. I hope that a year from now I'll be in the same position'."

But, in addition to hoping he'd be on the way home in a year, he wondered if in a year he'd look as old as those men looked.

He was given some in-country training before joining B2-7 during the last half of November. One of the things he was told to do was "to forget everything you learned in the States. We'll teach you how to survive. We'll tell you what this is all about."

Sayre was flown to a forward LZ, LZ Sue, to join the company. He was assigned to Holtz's squad in the 2nd Platoon. Gast was the platoon sergeant. Snag was a machine gunner. There was an assistant gunner, and Sayre was the ammo bearer. Sayre learned that for him to become the gunner, the current gunner and assistant gunner had to either get killed, wounded, or finish his tour of duty and go home.

There were things Sayre learned as he got acclimated to his new environment.

"When I first joined the guys at LZ Sue, moving from one location to another was called a 'hump'. Preparing for my first hump, I remember an old-timer telling me to get rid of my flak jacket and to get rid of my underwear. I'm thinking to myself, 'There's no fucking way. I'm civilized. I'm going to wear my underwear and my flak jacket'. Well, after that first three-kilometer hump, I was so soaked with sweat and my ass was so chaffed from the underwear that I dumped the flak jacket and didn't wear underwear for the rest of the year. He was a short timer and took the flak jacket. The flak jackets were heavy and hot. He knew what he was talking about."

Sayre's first real initiation to combat was not until early December when B2-7 went to help a sister company of the Battalion. D Company, which was Gast and Beierman's original assignment, had gotten mauled.

"My first action was a combat assault into a hot LZ. A hot LZ meant we were drawing fire going in as our helicopters approached. D Company (D2-7) was surrounded and had sustained heavy losses of twenty-five killed and fifty-two wounded. Charlie Company 2-7 went in first, and we followed. Drawing fire while going in, the choppers would not land but would skim the ground—and you had to jump out. I landed on top of a dead NVA who had the top of his head blown off. That was my first impression of combat. I still see him to this day. It looked like he had been hit right between the eyes."

Paul Decker, who had thought he would become a helicopter pilot, arrived at Cam Ranh Bay, Vietnam, just before Thanksgiving 1968. He was infantry. He received a three-day "refresher" course, did some guard duty, and had the pleasure of a detail burning shit with diesel fuel. From Cam Ranh Bay, he was sent to B2-7. Eventually, Decker made his way to the field where he met very briefly with his company commander who made it clear that there were two things to concentrate on: staying alive and killing the enemy. He was assigned to a squad in the 1st Platoon, B2-7. Decker was joined a few days later by another new arrival.

Jack "Squirt" Miller

Jack "Squirt" Miller arrived in Vietnam within days of Decker and was sent to the 1st platoon.

"I arrived at the company and had a quick meeting with the CO. He poured some orange juice into a canteen and told us there were three things we had to do. Stay alive, kill gooks, and go home."

With that, it was off to his new home with his platoon. Miller spent 90% of his time as the assistant machine gunner and the other 10% of the time as the actual gunner.

Decker's early weeks in the field were true eye-openers. He didn't realize he'd be walking point with little or no experience of having been in a firefight or without any familiarity about the way the NVA operated.

"What they did was they took away your M16 and gave you a 12-gauge shotgun, at least in my case they did. My first day on point I had the daylights scared out of me. At Cam Ranh Bay during the Vietnam orientation at Camp Alpha, the featured film was John Wayne and the Green Berets. All these bamboo points stabbing me every step, that's what was on my mind. Anyway, the CO got very upset because the point was moving so slow. It was bottlenecking everybody. A hundred twenty guys walking in a line through the jungle. The guys at the end are either sitting down or running so Lt. Montgomery walked up to me and said, 'What's wrong with you?' I said, 'I don't like this 12-gauge shotgun. I wasn't trained with one. I want the M16 back.' They gave me back my M-16, and things picked up from there."

With new faces throughout the company, the company was changing in late fall of 1968. From an operational and command perspective, that change had already begun. No one knew, yet, that there would be more changes, and it would seem, at the beginning, a bit bizarre and strange to the young guns who were already in the fight.

CHAPTER 4

WHAT'S GOING ON?

S gt. Hall, having completed DI school and successfully arguing his case to be assigned as a DI, made his way to a basic training company at Ft. Ord. He went, as ordered, to Company A, 1st Brigade and reported to the company commander.

"You're assigned to us, but you're going to go across the quadrangle and you're going to work for Delta Company. So, go over there and report to 1st Sergeant Trainer."

Hall went, though once again, it was a verbal order. There were no papers. Without considering the possible consequences, he did as ordered and headed to Delta Company.

"I went to work for Top. I got there about December 10, '67. I watched the platoon that was just finishing its training. I think they had to have been in their last week. And I just sort of bounced around. I was too late to really get involved with a group of trainees that had been working under other drill sergeants for seven weeks. I was just sort of an observer more than anything else."

Given the timing of the training cycles, the fact that D Company's trainees were finishing up their basic in mid-December meant some down time leading into the holidays. Ft. Ord seemed to close down.

"Top told all of us to take off, stay in town. If we had to leave town, call the CQ and get permission if you were going to leave town.

"I was living off post by that time with Bunny. Everything was just going great. Here, I had my Smokey Bear hat [hats DIs wore were derisively called "Smokey the Bear" hats], but I was wearing civvies. It was like being on leave, but I wasn't using any leave."

Everything was going fine. The timing of several things had worked out well for Hall. His drill sergeant course had ended late in the fall, his arrival at the basic training company at nearly the end of the cycle gave him time to observe, and the holidays had provided time for leisure, spending time with his wife.

There was a slight change in luck on Christmas eve.

"Three or four o'clock in the afternoon, my home phone rang in my little apartment in Seaside. It was Top. He says, 'Sgt. Hall, I have a problem'. I said, 'Yes, Top'. He says, 'I only have two people that can pull CQ from 1800 today till 1800 tomorrow'."

"I said, 'Yes, Top.' He says, 'The two people that can pull CQ are you and me, and it ain't going to be me'."

Sgt. Hall understood. He changed out of his civvies and into his fatigues. His mother-in-law, who was there for the holidays, gave him a strange look.

"What are you getting into your uniform for?"

"I've been called into work."

"You can't go to work. It's Christmas Eve."

"Well, I've just been ordered into work. So, I'm going into work."

"That's not right."

"Would you rather I be in Vietnam, right now? Or would you rather that I go to work and sit behind a desk for 24 hours?"

Put that way, Sgt. Hall's mother-in-law understood immediately. Top, having spent the previous Christmas in Vietnam, spent Christmas Eve and Christmas Day at home in 1967 with his wife and three sons. When he made that call to Sgt. Hall, Top had no idea that it would be three years before he would spend another Christmas at home with his family.

After the holidays, Sgt. Hall, as a DI, got his first batch of trainees in January 1968. Hall's platoon of trainees performed better than the other platoons on a consistent basis throughout the cycle. Hall's first platoon of trainees finished basic training, and it was on to the next group of trainees, often made up of mostly draftees. When he got his second batch of trainees, he knew something was "screwy".

"Normally, everything was alphabetical . . . I had these names from all over the place. I'm looking at this. . . . So, I'm looking at this, and I'm thinking that there's no rhyme or reason to this. I went down and I said, 'Top, obviously you know I'm going to train whoever you assign me. I'm just curious why do I have these names all over the alphabet?'"

"You'll figure it out," Top said.

"It took me about three or four days. They were a bunch of educated, athletic people who flunked out of school."

Hall's second cycle of trainees included a college football running back who had flunked out, a professional tennis player, entertainers, and, generally, an assortment of accomplished young men. Hall found out that Top had gone through the list of new recruits and decided to give Hall a platoon of trainees who might have been able to easily outwit a DI with only a high school diploma or GED. Hall, having a graduate degree, was seen as more capable to deal with them.

Although Hall was working hard and his trainees were performing well to reflect his work, he sometimes wondered if anyone noticed. Early during his time as a drill sergeant, he went in to ask Top a question. Top stayed behind his desk when Hall went in to see him.

Top looked at Hall and said, "You know, Fred, you're a pretty smart guy. Have we given you the necessary training to do your job?"

"Oh, yeah, yeah, sure, Top," Hall answered.

"And, are we giving you what you need to do your job, the resources to do it?"

"Oh, sure," Hall said.

"Then, get the hell out of here and go do your job."

Hall's hard work was being noticed. Hall's ability to get the most out of his trainees and having his trainees out-performing the trainees in other platoons led to his promotion to Staff Sergeant around the time his third cycle was ending. Despite only seventeen months in the Army, Hall had made rank quickly.

"It was a lot because of the way Top handled me. He was fond of saying, 'just another name on a roster'. But, he knew the different personalities that went with those names. He had the ability to bring out the best in people, whatever that best might be."

By August 1968, Hall had run trainees through basic training for several cycles. Another young NCO in the company had finished Drill Sergeant school. Top told Hall that he'd be taking a cycle off from being a drill instructor and doing more administrative work in the company. Top explained to Hall that it would be good for the newly minted drill instructor to have his own platoon for a cycle.

Hall accepted the change, understanding that a new DI would want his own platoon to run through basic training and Hall would simply switch duties and be the Training NCO. It sounded fine, having regular work hours.

It took several days, but Sgt. Hall finally realized why the switch of duties had occurred. He learned that there was an Inspector General inspection scheduled. That meant a pile of books and records for the company had to be put in proper order. Hall was finally realizing that there was always a reason behind the things Top did. Given Hall's academic bent, he was the right guy to get the company's paperwork in order for the upcoming inspection.

When the calendar hit late August or around Labor Day 1968, Hall had surgery. When he returned to duty, 1st Sergeant Trainer was no longer his first sergeant. Top was preparing for another tour in Vietnam. Hall worked for 1st Sgt. Trainer for a mere nine months.

It was the Army. They each had their duties, and separately, they carried on. The Army needed combat proven senior NCOs and 1st Sergeant Trainer fit that need. By 1968, the Army had been churning through experienced, senior NCOs, and because of the loss of men, the Army had turned to the instant NCOs, otherwise known as shake-and-bakes to fill their needs.

The Trainer family moved, but this time, not far. A fence separated Ft. Ord and Seaside, California. Though the actual distance between on-post housing and the house in Seaside may have been a few miles, it may as well have been a continent away. Again, I faced a new neighborhood, a new school, and new faces, all the result of the short move.

We prepared for another year.

The map of Vietnam was taped to the kitchen wall like it had been during the first tour. Generally, things would be the same as during the first tour. But, for me, there was one big difference. I started to believe that there was not going to be any happy ending this time around. My father had made it through Korea and his first tour in Vietnam. What were the odds? Then, two days before he was to leave, there was a "surprise" for me.

He told me my mother was pregnant. There was a lot of profanity bouncing around in my head as I listened to what he was telling me. It was a couple of days before my fifteenth birthday, and all I was thinking was how my life was screwed to the max.

CHAPTER 5

LIVES IN THE BALANCE

Pops, at times, had some interesting and random thoughts cross his mind while in Vietnam.

"I can remember being pinned down by a sniper and I said to myself, 'Oh, this is what the rabbit feels like'. I mean maybe normal people don't think like that. But, I wasn't thinking, well, he's going to kill me. It's like, 'Oh, that's what the rabbit feels like when a bunch of people shoot at him'."

Maybe some of those thoughts could be attributed to the heat and fatigue.

"I do remember I was out in the field one time walking through a rice paddy. Of course, you carry all that, got the ruck sack, three things of ammo. I was an assistant in the machine gun squad so I was carrying that and you're in this rice paddy, going through there. It's about a 120 degrees. You think crazy thoughts. And, I thought, 'God, you know, it'd be alright if I got shot right now'. Then, a round went off and I'm like, 'I didn't mean that, I was just joking'."

Pops had been with B2-7 for months when B2-7 moved south. It was a battalion-size move, involving several companies and hundreds of men. LZ Billy was a battalion-sized perimeter and had artillery at the center of the LZ. B2-7 worked out of LZ Billy. It was a strategic location near the Cambodian border. It was also in close proximity to the Ho Chi Minh trail where it re-entered South Vietnam from Cambodia.

November 2, 1968, was only the first or second day at LZ Billy and the 2nd Platoon of B2-7 was told to go out on a patrol. To Jack Jeter, it sounded simple enough. From what he heard, the platoon would go about 300 to 500 meters out from the perimeter, turn right or left, go about that same distance, and come back to the LZ. Sgt. Gast, a squad leader, was under a similar impression. The platoon was not supposed to go more than about 500 meters beyond the perimeter. The platoon's task was to sweep an area out in front of its position beyond the LZ's perimeter. Holtz, another squad leader in 2nd Platoon understood that "we were sent out on a 20-minute cloverleaf. There were gooks on every side of LZ Billy. They were all over the place, and we're still going to go out and fight them in a platoon? We still got sent out, just the 2nd Platoon."

With the mission in mind, Jeter took a canteen of water and a limited amount of ammunition: one bandoleer and only a handful of magazines. He decided he didn't need food or a pack. Gast thought the same, having one or two bandoleers and one or two canteens of water.

It did not go well.

Jeter recalls, "we took off walking out through the jungle out in front of us, and it wasn't real heavy vegetation at first."

Gast explains. "We went about three klicks. We went farther than what we were supposed to and, eventually, it was all jungle. We didn't know where we were."

Skinny had the best vantage point. He was walking point. It was the first time he and Holtz had really worked together.

"Basically, we got lost because the platoon leader, the lieutenant, couldn't read a map. We walked out, and we come across this trail. I stopped and told Holtz why I stopped. Holtz sends two machine gunners down the trail, maybe about ten feet. He starts looking for booby traps. He gets things secured and pulls out the radio and the lieutenant and Gast come up. There's a little conference, and we decide to keep going."

Jeter describes the patrol from his position in the column.

"We got out there a little bit. Skinny is walking point, and Edd Holtz is walking right behind him then . . . two or three people. I was walking point for my squad, but we're walking in a column. We go out there a little ways, and Skinny finds a trail. The lieutenant, the platoon leader, says, 'Hot damn, lets follow it.' And I'm thinking, 'Let's don't follow it.' I really wasn't into following trails."

Jeter is about the sixth or seventh man in the column. The trail was the undoing as it diverted them from the basic mission.

Skinny explains what happened next.

"I started out again and stopped again. Holtz asked, 'Why are you stopping,' and I said, 'there are three packs in front of me.' He brings up the guns again. He walks up a little ways, checks for booby traps again, and has me go to the front up on the trail. He pulls his bayonet and looks into the packs. They're filled with rice."

Finding the NVA packs, Holtz realized that this was not a good situation. "We knew we were close, and our shit was getting weak."

Skinny continues.

"Holtz then stands and points in a direction so I start walking and walk into a thick wall of bamboo. To me, they were forty or fifty feet tall. I'm from Oklahoma so I've never seen anything like this. The bamboo is seven, eight inches in diameter. It's a huge bamboo forest, and this trail goes through this bamboo in an "S" shape. Holtz is somewhere behind me. I turn out of this bamboo forest into sunlight, and there's a bomb crater right in front of me and sunlight. I'm standing on the edge of this, and the trail stops where the crater begins. I'm trying to look for a path around the bomb crater and see this man on the other side of the crater in a uniform."

From farther back in the column, Jeter describes what he saw.

"We take off and we're following this trail . . . Skinny calls back, a Vietnamese pack from the NVA soldier, had the red star on it, just lying on the side of this trail. I didn't pay much attention to it . . . because I thought there's gooks in the area. We walked on farther and we're moving slow and there was a lot of noise in the jungle that day. You could hear people doing things, like a clink or a thud from somebody dropping something or driving a pole into the ground or something. I'm thinking this doesn't sound right. We thought it was the noise from the LZ. Of course, it wasn't. We're walking along. We get to a bomb strike area, a bomb crater. We came out of the jungle off this Ho Chi Minh trail, which it had to be because there was woven bamboo on the ground. I'm looking right ahead and I see Skinny turn left and I see Edd turn left."

Skinny saw another soldier.

"He has a little green helmet on and a rifle across his chest. He has both hands on his hips looking at the crater just as I am. When I saw him, I waved and said, 'Hi, this is big fucking hole isn't it?' because I thought he was a South Vietnamese soldier. They told me in basic and AIT that they, the enemy, wore black pajamas and straw hats. He grabs the barrel of his rifle and pulls it off his shoulder. His eyes got as big as saucers, getting ready to pull off a round, and Holtz comes around and says, 'Who the fuck are you talking to?' Then all of a sudden, Holtz and the NVA see each other, and the NVA turns to run when Holtz gets him in the left temple."

Jeter saw it. "Holtz brings his 16 up to his shoulder and fires two shots and says, 'I got one' and I'm thinking, 'You got one what?'"

After the shooting, Gast recalls, "We immediately got up to where this guy was and went through his pack, got whatever information he had on him."

Jeter watched, thinking, "Oh, God, this ain't good." Jeter saw the lieutenant and Gast going through this guy's pockets and checking him out. "All I can think about is I'm looking at him, and he's still moving his hands, and his fingers are moving. Then, somebody said something about if there's one, there's bound to be more of them. We screwed around there for a few minutes."

Gast notes that "from that point, our platoon leader put all three squads on point. Holtz's squad stayed in the center. I was to the left walking point and a third squad to the right of Holtz. We had three squads, still in single file, walking, spread out, and we went probably fifty, seventy-five meters, maybe a hundred if that, and my point man took a round right in the chest, punctured his lung. He fell to the ground, and there was one other kid right behind him. When he went down, the medic ran up to him."

By this time, Jeter concludes that "the lieutenant didn't have a clue where we were." As the three squads walked separate columns, Jeter was walking point for the squad that was on the right side of Holtz's squad. "We get up into the jungle pretty far, and all hell breaks loose. Gast's point man is the first one hit. Well, actually, he's the only one hit in our group.

We all hit the ground, then we got into a little bit of a firefight."

Jeter remembers, "Guys are hollering, 'We're Americans, we're Americans' and I'm thinking, yeah, that's why they're shooting at us. Everybody thought we were still close to the LZ, and they thought we'd run into our own guys."

Gast's memory mirrors that of Jeter's. "We actually thought we'd walked into the perimeter of Billy. At first, when the gooks opened up on us we thought we were walking into Billy and that they were shooting at us. Guys were yelling, 'GI, we're GIs'." That explained why the NVA continued to shoot at them.

Jeter concludes that, "somebody called back to the LZ saying we needed help. We're on the ground trying to protect ourselves".

In addition to the bullets flying, grenades were thrown in their direction.

Unfortunately, while the medic was tending to Gast's wounded point man, the medic put his hand up and was shot through the hand.

"I sent another guy up while I was putting the rest of my squad on line. The medic was able to tell the other guy what to do. The medic couldn't do it because of his hand being shot. The round that took down my point man never came out the back so it stayed in him, but it punctured the lung. We put a piece of plastic over his lung. There really wasn't a lot of blood from it. In the meantime, I had a couple of guys make a stretcher out of fatigue shirts, something I learned in NCO School, so we cut a couple of branches down and made a stretcher."

What was not apparent at the outset was that the other units trying to get to the 2nd Platoon were making a bad situation worse. The NVA was positioned between the 2nd Platoon and the other American platoons and companies coming to the rescue. The 2nd Platoon was receiving fire from both the NVA and the Americans coming to their rescue.

"Between the gooks shooting at us and Bravo Company and Charlie Company shooting . . . we were under quite a bit of fire," Gast says.

Once the firefight started, Rich Dorsey remembers its intensity. "I remember not being able to lift up at all from a prone position. The firing was intense and low. We couldn't see the enemy, although they were just yards in front of us. We couldn't see them because of the jungle undergrowth. I was scared to death. I do remember the lieutenant and the platoon sergeant were nowhere in sight. They were useless. In the midst of the firing, I saw something coming over the jungle canopy. It couldn't have been twenty-five feet away. Then it dawned on me it was a grenade. I immediately yelled 'grenade'. The men around me scattered away from the grenade. It rolled directly toward me. There were stumps left from the NVA building their bunkers from the trees they cut down. I instinctively rolled over behind one of those stumps. The grenade blew up, and I was spared any injury."

In any war and during firefights, information is not always accurate. The 2nd Platoon had run into NVA. But if the troops going out to help the 2nd Platoon thought that there had been men killed and numerous wounded, then somewhere in the line of communication, things had gotten muddied.

Lt. Montgomery's 1st Platoon was sent out to help and rescue the 2nd Platoon.

"As I'm going out to get the 2nd Platoon, I'm thinking, why don't we have more guys going out here. We could certainly hear everything. They were throwing frags, and it was pretty intense. We got to maybe within a couple hundred, two hundred yards from them. We couldn't see because it was a jungle.

"The machine guns opened up on us. I would've cut the buttons off my shirt if I could've gotten lower. Somebody told me that there were more bullets passing over us during that firefight than when he was at Khe Sanh. I mean they [bullets] were inches over us because everybody was laying as quiet as they could lay and the machine gun bullets were going right over you. That's when the company commander started to stand up, and he got shot right between the eyes.

"Somehow, one of my machine gunners had managed to move up from the back to the front without his assistant gunner. Actually, he probably kept me from getting killed or captured because he stopped three NVAs that were flanking us and I couldn't get up to see what was going on and he managed to do that. And, he got the Silver Star for it. I don't think I'd be here today if it hadn't been for the machine gunner. That was just remarkable what he did," Montgomery explains.

The intensity of the NVA fire on the troops trying to help 2nd Platoon prevented a "rescue".

Jeter explains. "We're on one side, the gooks in the middle, and 1st Platoon on the other side. You've got this horrendous firefight going on, and it lasted a good 30-45 minutes. Of course, I ran out of water and was running out of ammunition. I'm thinking I better start saving bullets because I only had one bandoleer, and I was protecting our right flank. We stayed out there for quite a while, and 1st Platoon pulled back and said, 'You guys are going have to get out the best you can because we can't get to you'. I heard that on the radio myself."

Even though the troops trying to get to 2nd Platoon were unable to reach them, the 1st Platoon and others trying to reach them caused the NVA to divert their attention onto the additional American troops, relieving some of the pressure on 2nd Platoon.

Jeter believes that the NVA themselves started to pull back, leaving just a few troops to keep the Americans tied down. With the 1st Platoon and other American units unable to reach them, Gast said, "We finally started to pull back because the company couldn't get to us. We pulled back probably toward Cambodia because we were pretty close to the Cambodian border. We started to pull back. We put our wounded point man on the stretcher. When you picked it up, because it was made of shirts, it wasn't stiff enough so it just collapsed his shoulders together, pulling off the plastic that was on his chest. Finally, he said, 'You guys are killing me'. He got up and walked the rest of the way. And, he was holding the plastic on his chest. He was out of pain at least. He could walk."

As the 2nd Platoon was pulling back, somebody in a helicopter located the platoon, "he started calling in artillery in around us and got a Loach with a mini-gun on it and he just blew a path," Gast recalls.

What no one on the ground knew at the time was that a captain, in the helicopter above, was coordinating with the 2nd Platoon leader, arranging to create a path using a helicopter's mini-guns, to provide safe passage out. The captain flying overhead had been listening over the radio to the situation on the ground as he was headed to LZ Billy to take over another company and made a decision to help 2nd Platoon. The captain's helicopter brought him into the jungle where he organized the removal of the wounded before the rest of the platoon was taken out.

Jeter remembers that the Loach "got behind us and cleared us a trail out to a dirt road that I had no idea was there. It couldn't have been a hundred yards at the most. And we get out to this road."

Having reached a road and finding a clearing, Jeter watches, "here comes a slick in and off steps this guy, and I'm thinking who the hell is this guy." At that point, no one knew who had gotten off of the helicopter, he was unknown to anyone in 2nd Platoon. Ultimately, there were only two wounded in 2nd platoon, Gast's point man and the medic. The helicopter that had landed flew Gast's point man out.

Jeter recalls, "the first thing he says is you guys stick with me and I'll get you out of here."

Jeter, Gast and others wanted out, but they also had other needs after a firefight, spending time pinned down, and wondering if they would make it out.

Despite seeming to be out of danger, Jeter wasn't comfortable.

"The chopper took off, and it was deathly quiet. And we're standing on this road. It's pretty open and I'm thinking, 'Man, I don't like standing here'. This guy walked us down this road probably a 100 yards or so, and we turned into a grassy area where it looked like there used to be a hooch or something. We'd got so thirsty, I actually dug a hole in the ground and let water seep into it and then strained it with my bandanna and drank it because I was so thirsty."

Skinny, like the others, had left the LZ with only a canteen of water because of what he believed was going to be a short walk out and back into the LZ.

"We get to this opening and there are bomb craters and they're filled with water, bugs, and all this crap. We take our helmets and drink that water. We were thirsty, I've never been that thirsty in my life."

Gast's need for water equaled Jeter's and Skinny's.

"We're out of water and just about out of ammo cause we only took maybe a bandoleer or 2 bandoleers and one or two canteens and we were pinned down almost all day. We were out of water and filling our canteens up in bomb craters, which this new guy kept telling us not to do, but when you're thirsty and thinking, 'Who the hell is this guy,' not knowing who the hell he is . . . " They did not necessarily take the advice of someone they did not know even if he had gotten them out of their dire situation.

Second platoon did not have to walk back to LZ Billy.

"One chopper at a time landed picking up squads. The new guy from the helicopter came out on the last chopper . . . we landed on Billy and as we walked across Billy back to where our bunkers were on the perimeter, other companies were going 'Who the hell are you guys?' We said, 'Oh, we're 2nd Platoon, the ones you're trying to get'. 'Oh, no, you guys are all dead'. They thought we were replacements because the battalion commander supposedly called in for replacements because they weren't going to be able to get us," recalls Gast.

Jeter laughs as he thought about the return to LZ Billy.

"It took maybe a minute and a half to get back to the LZ. We were that close. It was a total screw up. If you want to see a cluster, that was it." During his first month in country up north, Jeter had not been in a firefight. "This was totally different. That's when I realized that this is not going to be a fun war. I think there's going to be more to it than camping and hiking." Jeter was correct as the days and months to follow would prove him right.

For someone like Jeter, an important lesson was learned.

"I had been out of water for a couple of hours and that was probably one of the worst feelings, that and not having any bullets. Didn't like that worth a damn. It never happened again. I always carried five quarts of water and every piece of ammo I could find. It ain't much fun running out of ammo or water, not in a firefight."

Sgt. Gast, who started the day as a squad leader in the 2nd Platoon, was one of those trying to survive the onslaught of machine gun fire from the NVA. Sgt. Holtz, another squad leader in the 2nd Platoon, was in the same predicament. Gast recalls that the platoon sergeant, who should have been trying anything to improve the situation, was simply in hiding mode as the platoon was under withering NVA fire.

An image of the platoon sergeant registered in Jeter's mind.

"During the firefight, I'd actually moved back to see if I could find some water and he was leaning up against a termite mound reading a magazine during the middle of a firefight. I'm like, 'Oh, maybe this isn't as bad as I thought it was'. I thought, 'No, wait a minute, it probably is as bad as I think it is'."

Sgt. Gast became a platoon sergeant. After returning to LZ Billy, he never saw his platoon sergeant again. Gast exercised his own judgment in deciding certain things once he became a platoon sergeant after the

November 2nd firefight.

"My responsibilities changed totally from being a squad leader. I started out with four squads. I eliminated the machine gun squad by putting a machine gun in each of the other squads because up north we'd go out on ambush and never take a gun with us. So, the squad would go out without a machine gun. I solved that problem."

With B2-7's loss of its company commander, the captain who had flown in to get the 2nd Platoon out became the new company commander on November 3rd. The new company commander, Barry McCaffrey, hit the ground running. Lt. Montgomery recalls that shortly after extricating 2nd Platoon of B2-7 from its grim situation, the company was volunteered to go help another company that was pinned down.

Captain McCaffrey, the new company commander, brought a new approach—an aggressive approach. Sgt. Holtz had not yet been in the country for two months, but noticed that for the guys who had been in Vietnam for many months and survived Khe Sanh, the A Shau and the Sands, they just wanted to make it to the end of their tours. They wanted to make it home. The question was, how to deal with a new company commander who wanted to find and engage the enemy?

It was not simply a change in a company commander but changes in tactics. Although Lt. Montgomery had not been in country that long, either, just since September, he did notice a difference when Captain McCaffrey took over. Having been a platoon leader since arriving in Vietnam, he noticed that on patrols the new CO used artillery and dropped rounds in front of the company as they moved in the jungle, which would make it easier to call in artillery in the event that it was needed. The new CO, while aggressive, was also careful.

"McCaffrey prepped LZs with artillery or airstrikes before going into the LZ. If an LZ was grassy, McCaffrey had it burned. They'd drop white phosphorous or whatever. It was another company in our battalion, their company commander took them into an LZ with tall grass and if there was either VC or NVA around that field somewhere, they lit it on them. Some guys were burned, munitions were cooking off, and they dumped all their stuff and were just running. Some of them didn't even have guns. They just threw their stuff down and ran because it was a wild fire. We never had that. McCaffrey prepped those LZs before we got there."

For a young lieutenant like Montgomery, another noticeable difference was that McCaffrey spent more time with his platoon leaders, the young lieutenants, to teach them. McCaffrey was aggressive, but he also taught them how to decrease risk while being aggressive.

There were a number of things that changed, but not all of them made the men of B2-7 happy. Jerry Gast also noticed an immediate difference. His new company commander seemed to volunteer the company for every mission possible. Only a few days after his platoon was pinned down, the company was out on another patrol.

"We went out about a klick and a half and came back in the dark. Nobody was very happy or thrilled with McCaffrey over that. It was so dark we had to hang on to the guy in front of us on the way back. You couldn't even see the guy in front of you."

And, of course, there were those occasions when B2-7 was volunteered to help rescue another company in trouble. McCaffrey volunteered the company to get D Company out of a hot situation, Gast recalls.

"D Company walked into a bunker complex and couldn't get back out. We went out with only half the company. We flew into a hot LZ right at dusk. We were told we'd walk them out that night, but that didn't happen.

"Dorsey was in my squad. We were sitting in the chopper and could see tracers fired at us and one of them hit near the door gunner. We were getting off the helicopter, and McCaffrey was on the ground like he was welcoming us to a party, directing guys where to go. We had no packs, no entrenching tools, but we had a lot of ammo. We laid on the ground that night, couldn't dig in."

Gast remembers that there was a memorable moment that night. "After a couple of hours, word was being passed around the perimeter that someone was watching the NVA pull out, moving out their wounded, and they'd counted that up to a hundred had walked by them and no one had started shooting at them. When word got to McCaffrey, all you heard was him screaming, 'don't count them, shoot'em!'

"Next morning, we walked D company out. The wounded went out on choppers. The next night, they called in a B-52 strike to bomb the bunker complex, which was only about a klick from the LZ. We couldn't hear the planes. They had strobe lights in the center of the perimeter for the pilots. All of a sudden, you could hear the bombs, squealing, whistling sound of the bombs, and the next thing it lit up the sky and we got out of our bunkers because we were afraid they would cave in on us. Then, within minutes, everything went black because the dirt from the B-52 strike was falling on us. The next morning, McCaffrey volunteered us to go back into the bunker complex and assess the damage. You could walk from one bomb crater to the next. It was carpet bombed about a klick wide and klick long."

Everybody learned quickly that McCaffrey was going to keep his company active. But, at least they avoided getting into firefights with other companies in their own battalion, which is what happened to Companies A and C who left LZ Billy and started shooting at each other and tried to call in artillery only to be told that they were shooting at each other.

While the aggressive nature of the new company commander took some getting used to, he did know what he was doing. Despite some things that may have been distasteful, B2-7's fate was moving in a positive trajectory.

CHAPTER 6

BARS AND STRIPES

Thanksgiving 1968 was approaching. First Sergeant Trainer had left his basic training company duties at Ft. Ord and had resettled his family just off post in Seaside, California. By the time the long holiday weekend arrived, he had already departed for his second tour of duty in Vietnam.

He was closing in on the twenty-year mark, having joined the Army at seventeen and finding himself in Korea weeks after the war broke out in 1950. He experienced combat at the ripe young age of eighteen. He had endured the brutal cold of Korea and had already felt the heat and humidity of Vietnam's tropical weather during his first tour of duty in Vietnam down in the Mekong Delta area. He was in for the long haul and about to endure another year of jungles and tropical heat and humidity.

For the men of B2-7, an overwhelming number of them were draftees or "volunteered" for the draft. To the extent that any could be considered "regular army," most, if not all, had very little time in the army. The young NCOs had gotten their stripes quickly.

Lt. Montgomery admitted that the best platoon sergeant he had during his seven months in the field was a nineteen-year old "shake-and-bake" Dale Beierman. The three other platoon sergeants who had been career army were doing as little as possible to get their year in, go home, and get to the twenty-year mark so they could retire. Despite his OCS course, the jungle course, and platoon leader duties stateside, the Lieutenant's interactions with first sergeants had been minimal. First of all, first sergeants often did not place much stock in 2nd lieutenants and so Montgomery had little to do with the First Sergeant when he was an officer in a basic training company. He observed that the First Sergeant seemed to hate trainees, watching the First Sergeant take a deliberately hardened hat and tap trainees on the nose, probably just to annoy or intimidate them. On arrival at B2-7 in Vietnam, he could not remember ever meeting the First Sergeant.

Sgt. Gast had witnessed the uselessness of his career platoon sergeant during the November 2nd firefight. He had no contact with a first sergeant except in rear areas. "We thought they were supposed to stay in the rear." On occasion, the company would get a break of a day or two from the field. "A two-day drunk," Gast explains.

As for first sergeants, Gast's impression was shaped by his first sergeant in the rear who ran the bar. The First Sergeant, who had a pet monkey, would get drunk.

"He'd get drunk, and the monkey would get drunk and be running up above the rafters and the First Sergeant would get mad, pulled out a .45, and shot holes in the roof. That was the contact I had with the First Sergeant."

Sgt. Holtz, in the same platoon as Gast, shared the same feelings as Gast concerning his first platoon leader, a lieutenant, and his initial platoon sergeant. Holtz, who was a squad leader, had no idea what to expect from either first sergeants or company commanders because he had not had any direct contact with them stateside. Other than having more rank, he did not know what they were supposed to do. He had no real frame of reference. To some extent, he thought first sergeants stayed in rear areas and got lazy sitting back there. His impression was shaped by career platoon sergeants he had already seen who stayed in the back of formations in the field or sat around reading magazines while the bullets were flying.

The sentiment regarding the platoon sergeant seemed to be shared widely as Jack Jeter's impressions were the same as those of Gast and Holtz. Jeter had heard that there was a new first sergeant joining the company, but given his experience to that point, which was not all that long, he just thought, "great to get another useless lifer".

The reality was that after entering the Army none of these men interacted with anyone with rank or if they did, it was very limited. They routinely dealt with junior NCOs and junior officers if they interacted with them at all.

Jesse "Pops" Groves had been in Vietnam for seven months. His view was that anyone above the rank of Staff Sergeant (an E-6) "seemed to find ways not to be there," meaning in the field where the fighting was done.

"I never saw him, you get to the rear I guess you'd see him, but I never, I don't ever remember seeing a first sergeant in the field till Top got there."

Pops couldn't be sure that he had seen a first sergeant in the rear.

Jon "Snag" Johnson, who had been in Vietnam since June, felt that there had not been anything memorable about senior NCOs.

It was safe to say that for the young combat weary men in B2-7, any new arrivals who were senior or career NCOs might have to prove themselves before getting the benefit of the doubt. Impressions already etched in the minds of those who had been in country would be hard to change. To them, career NCOs had the reputation of either doing little to nothing useful or doing more harm than good.

It was either the very end of November or the beginning of December when 1st Sergeant Trainer got to B2-7.

Gast remembers, "I was shocked when he showed up like 'what the hell is the first sergeant doing out here in the field' because I thought they all stayed in the rear and I thought 'this guy's nuts, what's he doing out here'. Because I was the platoon sergeant, he was making his way around, interacting with all the platoon sergeants to get to know them."

Pops' initial impression was, "don't know if he's smart or what because he didn't need to be out there." His implication was that perhaps they had someone whose sanity needed to be checked. In the beginning, seeing the first sergeant out in the field and going on patrols, "it freaked me out."

All Snag knew was that they suddenly had this "older person" out there in the field and wondered where he came from. He didn't know what to think.

Snag did hit on one thing. The new first sergeant was "older." He was the oldest man in the company. For someone like Snag, who had just entered the Army in January at the age of nineteen, his new first sergeant may have seemed ancient, being nearly twice as old as he was—seventeen years his senior. And, probably, his new first sergeant looked older in other ways. After months of pounding away in the hills and jungle heat, Snag was leaner than he was when he first arrived whereas the first sergeant was filled out, not quite six feet, but broad shouldered and had bulk.

The arrival of the new first sergeant was only a few weeks after getting the new company commander on November 3rd, after the "lost platoon" incident. If they thought things had changed with the new CO, more changes, some seemingly strange at first, were going to occur.

If the mere presence of a first sergeant in the field caused Sgt. Gast to wonder about the mental state of this new guy, other things that the new first sergeant did simply re-enforced the concern.

"Being on patrol and him walking with a point platoon, it's like, 'this guy's crazy and sometimes with the point squad to see how they reacted'."

The extremes of what he had experienced in the past and what he was witnessing with the new first sergeant were hard to reconcile at first.

But, as Sgt. Gast learned, what appeared initially to be madness or perhaps something slightly less than that was simply Top's way of doing things.

Initially, these questions bounced around in the heads of a number of guys.

Pops admits, "it shocked me. Because I'd been over there all this time and I hadn't seen a first sergeant in the field and he comes out there and he even goes on patrols with you. So, I'm thinking, 'Who is this guy'?"

Pops acknowledges that he thought maybe he had a crazy first sergeant because why be out in the field if he didn't have to be there.

"I never heard of any first sergeant that stayed very long in the field. I don't blame them. If I made first sergeant, you think I'd be out there?"

The fact that, for the most part, these men had never witnessed the sighting of a first sergeant in the field raised some suspicion.

It didn't take long for perceptions to change. There were different perceptions of how much the new first sergeant was in the jungles with his company. But, regardless of those different perceptions, one thing that became clear was that the new first sergeant was out there with them.

Quickly, Sgt. Gast, the 2nd Platoon's platoon sergeant, learned that what appeared initially to be madness became the new normal.

"Top arrived and interacted with the platoon sergeants to get to know them. He would go around and talk to all of us. He wanted to see how point platoons and point squads reacted."

Gast got to know his new first sergeant better when both were at a forward LZ.

"We sat down and talked. We got our hot beers and were sitting there just talking near the mortar platoon while they were shooting mortars off. About the third beer, there was a short round that came right back. We got up, walked over, and took a look at the short round. It was bright red. He says, 'We probably should get away from this in case it goes off'."

Gast was not an exception.

"Top did that with every platoon sergeant and got to know them and worked his way around and got to know all the squad leaders. So, he spent a lot of time in the field. He'd disappear and go to the rear every now and then, but would be back there maybe a couple of days and come back. He'd go straighten things out back there and then come back, because of issues with supplies. He'd go back to find out why we weren't getting supplies we needed."

"He interacted with the platoon sergeants mostly and then the squad leaders. If he wasn't walking with the platoon, he was walking with the command CP, with Six [McCafffrey]. So I would see him. He'd call all the platoon sergeants up to the CP when all the lieutenants were talking with Six," Gast remembers. "He was out there, in the field, a lot."

"It drastically changed the way the company performed. Top and McCaffrey coming in the November, December time frame, compared to the type of company we were, most of us wouldn't be alive if it wasn't for these two because we had no real leaders. McCaffrey controlled the lieutenants in the company, and Top controlled the platoon sergeants to make sure they were doing their jobs right. The priorities all of sudden became keeping everybody alive, but still doing your job. Having a first sergeant who wasn't afraid to be up front, at least from a platoon sergeant's perspective, it was like, you felt more relaxed or, well, not safer, but if he's crazy enough to be out here I guess the rest of us should be doing what we're supposed to be doing. It was his leadership that made it easier for everybody to do what we were doing. He backed his platoon sergeants."

The focus on getting everybody through their tour of duty was a 24/7 effort. If McCaffrey had brought about a sense of improved tactics during the day. He and Top were also focused on the night. A secure perimeter in the field at night meant attending to details.

"Six and Top would both walk the perimeter at different times and check on everything. Make sure everything was in place. Top would do one for sure if Six was busy. He would always be out checking the perimeter, stop and talk to the squad leaders and platoon sergeants," Gast explains.

The way the McCaffrey-Top tandem worked was not what Gast had expected and took some getting used to in the field.

"Top was with the point platoon about half the time. Otherwise he was with the command CP, which is where he was supposed to be from my perspective. When I was running the platoon, that's when I realized McCaffrey was with the point platoon and not back where he's supposed to be either. He says, 'If I'm not up here, I can't see what's going on'. He'd walk right behind my radio operator. Top would do the same thing when he was up there."

Gast describes the interesting interaction that could occur when his platoon was on point.

"Funny thing about McCaffrey, I'd turn around to tell him something and he'd say, 'Use your radio,' and we're only five, ten feet apart. At the time, it was all business."

Gast adapted to the new way things were being done and, while it was very different, it had a positive impact and result.

Holtz, who was in Gast's platoon, had two and a half months in country and was a squad leader when Top arrived in B2-7. He had no recollection of any previous first sergeant in Vietnam, but remembers that when Top arrived, "he was always concerned about our stuff, our welfare, what we needed. What did we need to make things better?"

There were material needs of the men in the field to address, but Top also needed to gauge how his young NCOs performed in the field. For

Holtz, who had no frame of reference about first sergeants, it provided a different perspective.

"He'd walk point with me. He'd back me up walking point, and he did it with everybody just to know his squad leaders. It was very important to him. It didn't seem strange at all for him to walk point. This was business. It was business with a man, like when you have a coach, a mentor, a superior, that you don't look at so much as a superior by rank, but someone that you just want to please, someone whose respect you want, someone you want to show what you can do because you want things right with him. For me, it was like, 'Wow, Top's coming today, going to be with us walking point.' It was my chance to show him, you have a good squad leader leading a combat toughened squad. I want to please you. We want this to go well. It's like the coach sending you out, and you wanting to do well to reward his confidence in you. I liked walking point. For the opportunity to 'show off' couldn't wait. He'd have a .45 and a double-bladed ax and a towel around his neck. With his sparkling blue eyes, his wide smile matched my smirk. Time for business brought a different look. I'd give my point man a nod, and 2nd squad would lead the company out."

"When the first sergeant came, he was always in the field with us," Lt. Montgomery recalls, having had little contact with first sergeants up until this time. "As soon as the bullets started flying, he was moving up, he was going to the front to get with McCaffrey."

Montgomery recounts that "Top had more contact with McCaffrey than me because I'm with my platoon. I'd go to where McCaffrey was and wherever he set up his little group for the night. We'd all, platoon leaders, go over there in the morning and with the first sergeant, we'd have our little meeting. We would go on patrol, and you'd go single file through the jungle. You did that all day. McCaffrey might call you over, along with the first sergeant, at night to talk about something. But, mostly, it was digging foxholes and setting up the perimeter, getting the claymores out and the flares and that kind of thing.

"The first sergeant mostly worked with the platoon sergeants. And, McCaffrey worked with his lieutenants so I would see the first sergeant to say 'hi' every now and then, but he wouldn't be in my platoon area at night. I didn't leave my platoon area at night. I was there with my guys."

Though he may have worked mostly with the platoon sergeants because he oversaw his younger NCOs, it didn't mean he wasn't aware of the need to ensure that his young lieutenants progressed in learning the craft of soldiering.

"We all looked to Top for guidance at some point. He'd help us with things we were concerned with. When I went to Vietnam, I'd never called in artillery. That's pretty important so he would help us with things like that, where there were gaps in our training," Montgomery recalls.

"We left OCS with a lot of gaps. I never worked with a tank, but I got to sit in a tank and then get out of it. That was the extent of tank training. I had no idea how mortars worked. There were just these gaps. In fact, they told the company I was in at OCS, they didn't have time to teach us everything so if you weren't a quick learner you were dead. During OCS, if you were sick or couldn't go to the field, there was no repeat. He was a great teacher. We certainly looked to him for guidance."

Michael McMahan

Lt. Michael McMahan, B2-7's forward artillery observer (FAO), had arrived in Vietnam in August '68. He believed that the company's first sergeant at that time was simply marking time. He witnessed a significant change in the company with McCaffrey's arrival and the addition of Top. Although McMahan's time under McCaffrey and with Top was extremely short, less than six weeks in the company after Top's arrival, both left lasting impressions.

"One thing I remember well about Top, he was especially good at managing young, junior officers like me. He was military respectful, too much so, in my mind, but he had a knack for telling me that I needed a little improvement in what I was doing and how I was doing it. In other words, sometimes I was acting like a second lieutenant. But what I liked is that he did not make me feel stupid, though I most certainly was. He would just stand up, walk over to me, sometimes with bullets flying all over the place and say, '28 (my call sign) follow me and I'll help you find a better observation point'. In other words, the bottom of a foxhole with my hands over my head might not be the best place to call in artillery. He had a way of instilling confidence, and he and McCaffrey never showed fear. In a fire fight, Top and McCaffrey would divide up and go to the most vulnerable locations and get everybody doing their jobs. I never saw Top rip off his shirt, put a bayonet in his teeth, and charge the NVA with a .45, but he simply went to where we were vulnerable, organized the men properly and made sure everybody was on mission. He was a leader, and he and McCaffrey were a terrific leadership team."

"We were in almost constant firefights November through Christmas Day 1968," McMahan recalls.

"McCaffrey and Top formed an amazing team. Every company in the battalion was experiencing massive casualties, many, many killed including two FAO's like me . . .2 out of 4. McCaffrey and, then a week or so later, Top taught us how to fight and do it with fewer casualties. It was basic infantry 101. When you are hit, respond with overwhelming firepower. Use everything in your arsenal. For me artillery. For the grunts, rapid controlled small arms, M-60s, grenades. We learned to throw them in sync concentrating the effect. I was given freedom to coordinate the aerial assaults with gunships, F-4s, Cobras, even C130s with Gatling guns. We never went backwards. We plowed into and over the enemy. McCaffrey even got a bugle, and we blew it as we poured everything we had on the NVA. Result: though the other companies were experiencing high KIAs, we had no one killed in November and December to my knowledge, though we were continually in the shit. Two men were primarily responsible for that outcome: Captain McCaffrey and First Sergeant Trainer."

Lt. Montgomery realized that in addition to the first sergeant's teaching abilities, there were other traits that were exhibited that were not as welcoming.

"He could say 'Lieutenant' where it stung."

Montgomery also became aware of the way Top could throw a look in your direction that sent a clear message, whether it was a chill or fear that the look instilled.

"I learned that when he gave you 'the look' you just needed to be somewhere else. I got the look once or twice when he first got there. He was a good teacher, and he helped in his own way to guide us."

Montgomery remembers clearly one incident that invited the look.

"He did get really mad at me once. It was really hot that day with no breeze and just humid. It was brutal. I looked at him. We'd been marching through the jungle. That's a chore. Somehow, I ran into him that day because usually, he wouldn't walk up front. McCaffrey would be up front, and he'd be a platoon or two back. I looked at him, and he just didn't look right. He was really beet red in the face and just didn't look like himself. I got the medic to go check on him. The medic came back and told me that his blood pressure was really high so I told McCaffrey and we got him evac'd out. He was very mad at me for getting him out of the field. Most people would be fine getting a hot meal, shower, but no, he didn't want to leave. That's one time I did get the look."

It was almost as if he needed, at times, to be ordered out of the field. An order that, if given to most of the men of B2-7, would be happily received and obeyed. Top's personal traits were leaving a mark on Lt. Montgomery.

"He was the finest first sergeant I ever worked with. He was an expert infantry first sergeant. There was no one more courageous."

Dale Beierman, a squad leader in 1st Platoon under Montgomery, did not have much interaction with Top, but one thing that did stand out was that "as far as leadership qualities, he was certainly observing us. He pegged us. He knew what our leadership styles were like." At least to Beierman, Top's assessments were dead-on accurate and made him wonder "how the hell did he know that?" Then again, Beierman noted that "Top was very well aware of what was going on. I was just aware of the first platoon. He knew his men, knew them well, spending time with them."

For those who were not squad leaders or platoon sergeants, their interaction with Top was very limited. Generally, men lived and operated within their own squads and platoons. That was their world.

Jon "Snag" Johnson had been in Vietnam for over five months when Top arrived. But, being with the gun squad, and not being a squad leader, he had limited direct contact with the new CO and first sergeant. Despite the little contact, he sensed an improved morale.

"Top was out there, before it got dark. He'd go around the perimeter." The one thing Snag did notice was that "Top was all business, not just putting in time when in the field with us, there was a presence about him that there was no fooling around out there."

Jack Jeter was not a squad leader or platoon sergeant when Top arrived in Vietnam. He realized that Top spent a good amount of time in the field and noticed Top walking with the 2nd Platoon and the squads within the platoon. He also saw that Top went around to ensure that things were set up for night security.

Jeter's contacts with Top increased after his February 1969 squad leader's course. Once he was elevated to squad leader, he participated in the regular "meetings" that covered the next day's mission.

Chris Sayre and Paul Decker arrived in B2-7 only days apart in late November. McCaffrey had been the CO of the company for only a couple of weeks when they arrived and their arrival was shortly before the arrival of 1st Sergeant Trainer. Sayre's impression was that Top seemed to be second in command more so than people thought because the lieutenants didn't really know what was going on. Top, being older and more experienced than the lieutenants, was more in command than the other officers. Top didn't simply stay with the CO or radio operators, but was more interactive with all the elements of the company.

Decker's interactions with Top were strictly business. To some extent, the reason why he didn't see much of Top was the way the platoons rotated walking point and the location of the CP group within the line of the company.

"I saw Top more in the evenings because he would walk around the perimeter and inspect it when guys were in their fox holes. When he was in the field, he routinely walked the night perimeter."

To many who had been in the company before November '68, they sensed a significant change in B2-7 toward the end of the year. Objectively, it might be hard to say whether they were "safer," but psychologically, as Gast describes it, there was a stronger feeling that their new leadership team was better equipped to get them through whatever they encountered.

Rich Dorsey, who had been in Vietnam for five months by the time Top arrived, was in a good position to see how things changed, having been under other COs and NCOs in the company. As McCaffrey's radio operator, RTO, Dorsey saw the leadership team in action.

"Great leaders exude that respect that you want to give them because you recognize they had it together. McCaffrey had it. You could sense a difference with him. The other CO was fine, but he was not a McCaffrey, without a doubt. McCaffrey was definitely above anyone else and then when Top came in, it was like the total leadership was there. It was like, what a difference." For Dorsey, with the two men in place, "It was a difference of night to day. Not only in terms of discipline, in structure, in strategy, but also in terms of emotional uplift."

"I saw Top in the field a lot," Dorsey recalls. "He and McCaffrey, they didn't lead by pushing us, they led by example. You wanted to do what they wanted done. McCaffrey came across as the father figure, do this, don't do that. Of course, McCaffrey wasn't verbose, he says what he wants in a few words and that's it. He doesn't have to explain things. You just do it. What Top brought was, in a tough way, firm way, brought the other side of the marriage environment, while he was tough and you didn't play around with either one, he could soften what McCaffrey's directives were in such a way, still without a lot of words, but he would handle them with a quietness and yet the firmness, that you go, yeah, I understand. I'm with you, Top. It was such a wonderful blend, it was uncanny. I'm trying to equate it to a father and a mother and the different roles they played.

"I just constantly remember having to go save other companies in our battalion. Certainly, Company D, was the worst. It seems like they got all the rejects from all the other companies when they had to build the company back up and they continued to get hit because they didn't have the discipline and, perhaps, the leadership."

Dorsey contrasted that from B2-7.

"The routes that McCaffrey would take, totally by the book, not pleasant, not fun, because you wanted to go on the trail, but he knew that that was the riskiest place for any ambushes, booby traps, or anything. You knew, even though it wasn't pleasant, it was for your own good. And through the reassurance of Top, quiet, simple reassurance and the presence of Top, he's an incredibly smooth guy."

Personally, Dorsey found having Top in the field "was a settling thing. Now, we have someone constantly with us, constantly looking out for us, directing us, whatever, intervening as appropriate, taking McCaffrey's orders and defining them down to our level of what each of us had to do, were supposed to do. It was reassuring, totally reassuring. That's the feeling that I had of the two of them. I was so reassured while we went into garbage and some of what we ran into, a lot of what we ran into when we were trying to save other companies, or give them support, pull them out of some situations. There was a confidence they exuded that translated down to our positions like, yeah, this is what we're supposed to do. I'm not nervous at all. It was so easy. They made the directions, the orders so easy to understand that they, you knew they had a purpose. You quickly gave trust to McCaffrey and Top, and you just did what you were supposed to because you knew it was totally for your own good and would make total sense whether we knew it or not."

Edd Holtz realized that the benefits of having an experienced senior NCO was not just about having Top with the company in the field.

"Top was sitting by his hooch in the rear, and I went and sat with him. We started having these 'talks' and it strengthened a personal relationship. One of the topics we talked about was fear and the point was that I wasn't scared. I was trying to understand how to deal with men and people as a squad leader. So, I would spend time with Top and talk about lots of different things, things that had nothing to do with Vietnam, but about life."

Those serious 'talks' that had begun on the few occasions when Top and Holtz were in the rear allowed for lighter moments even when they were in the field.

"Skinny, once in the middle of sentence, looked at me, covered up his mouth, pointed at my upper lip and said 'You're trying to grow a moustache'. He saw all 11 light blond hairs above my lip. The next son of a bitch that was over at my foxhole taking a good close look at it was Top and that's where 'Baby-san' came from."

The nickname stuck, not just in Vietnam, but in the years since. At opportune moments nearly fifty years later, Top still refers to him as "Baby-san."

Holtz's decision about his R&R was another opportunity for Top to mess with him.

"I didn't take the R&R to Australia. It came about that they said to get some info on Holtz, he's going out to Australia at the end of April. They called and I said 'no, I'm going to Hong Kong in May'. So, whoever was on the other end says 'Fine.' They just hung up. Nobody told me there was something special. Nobody told me a damn thing. But, Top got around to coming around to my foxhole with his helmet over his heart with that big-ass, white-tooth smile and tells me what a sleazy Baby-san I was because I missed it and milked it for all it was worth for the next week or two until we got the Stars and Stripes with the guy that did take it and spent nine days all expenses paid with Miss Australia of 1968. He loved it."

Pops, who had been in Vietnam for seven months before McCaffrey took charge of B2-7 and about eight months before Top arrived, found it easy to divide his time in Vietnam into the "before" and "after." To Pops, the difference was noticeable after McCaffrey and Top arrived.

"Top and McCaffrey brought a lot of experience to the company. It was more gung-ho after McCaffrey arrived, but the leadership was different. We got into more 'stuff' in a shorter period of time, but McCaffrey and Top kept people together, knew what they were doing. We had good platoon sergeants and so we had a better team of leaders keeping people alive."

For Pops, seeing Top in the field was different than with the officers.

"I could relate to him. I've got more admiration for him than any of them. The way he conducted himself around us. He was always trying to help you do things. I thought he was the reincarnation of John Wayne. He was like the father figure."

As Pops notes, the company was seeing more engagement and getting into more firefights under McCaffrey than it had prior to McCaffrey taking command. There were efforts to give B2-7 breaks out of the field and time in the rear to relieve stress. Lt. Montgomery describes what happened on one of the occasions when the company was taken to the rear. It was to Quan Loi, the large battalion size LZ.

"It was like a three-day vacation, but really you're traveling two days. We came in there and the first night, we had showers, a hot meal, and then it got dark and everybody disappeared. The next day we were asked to leave Quan Loi to go back to the jungle where we belonged. We had to round up the guys because they were on the ground sleeping and just passed out all over the place. It was nuts. That was pretty embarrassing for McCaffrey."

Jeter recalls another occasion when he thinks the company was flown from Quan Loi to Tan Son Nhut, outside of Saigon for a three-day break.

"They put us on these large planes, like C 130s or something, and they parked the planes way out away from the terminal. They took us off the plane and marched us through the terminal. I'm seeing all these guys in spit shined boots and starched fatigues and no weapons and wondering, 'What the fuck is this? We're getting fucked'. Anyway, they turned us loose on this base that night. We were supposed to spend two or three days there, but they kicked us off the base the next day. It was a fiasco. We all got drunk. The next day, we did an air assault out of Tan Son Nhut, north of Saigon. We landed on a dirt road north of Saigon, and I felt so bad that when we landed, I just rolled over, crawled into a ditch, and went to sleep."

Under McCaffrey and Top, B2-7 fought hard and, obviously, played hard. They knew how to make up for the lack of casual time.

There was no doubt that B2-7 had changed significantly for those who had been in the company before November. For the more experienced, most felt that, though B2-7 seemed to be getting into more contact with the enemy, their odds of making it out had improved because of the added experience at the top and it filtered down through the company command structure. In any war zone where peace and quiet can transform abruptly into hell, the only question was: how long would B2-7 be able to keep its leadership team in place and be the recipient of good leadership and a bit of luck?

CHAPTER 7

BLOOD BROTHERS

With the flip of the calendar into a new year, time was getting close for Lt. Montgomery to be pulled out of the field. He had been a platoon leader since September.

"If you were with your platoon for four months, that was considered long enough and they'd take you out of the field. They had sent out two potential replacements that I worked with and turned them down."

A lingering question had to be, well, what happens to lieutenants who are rejected as a replacement platoon leader?

"One of them became the R&R officer in Australia," Montgomery answered.

It simply demonstrated the Army's sense of humor.

Montgomery did get a "safer" job, but it was in the field.

"At about six months, McCaffrey assigned me to the mortar platoon. The mortar platoon walked third, two platoons in front and one behind. That was safer because when there was contact, we would move the mortar platoon back to the last clearing we went through and set up the tubes and start firing rounds in support."

A conclusion to be drawn is that, at least in the case of B2-7, anyone sent out to take over a platoon was not going to be accepted if he didn't demonstrate some level of competence in the field, but therein lies the catch-22. After months in the field and learning what he needed to do to lead an effective fighting platoon, how would anyone be in a position to take over Montgomery's position with a similar level of skill? Although Montgomery stayed in the field with the mortar platoon, the mortar platoon did not walk in the point platoon position. In Vietnam, "safe" was a relative term. Walking in the jungles with two platoons in front of where you are in the column meant you were in a safer place.

January 18, 1969

"Somebody yelled for a machine gun. I was on the other side of the perimeter so I ran, jumped behind a mound, and started shooting," Snag remembers.

Jack Jeter looked over toward Snag. "I was no more than seven to ten yards from Snag. Snag was getting rounds all around him. I was getting nothing, absolutely nothing. I'm lookin' and lookin', trying to figure out where the fire's coming from. The jungle was so thick I couldn't tell."

"It's funny they didn't put me out of commission permanently," Snag recalls. He worked his machine gun. "Next thing I know, Holtz is crawling up my butt and says, 'Hey, you're bleeding,' and I said, 'No, it's just the hot sun.' Well, I was bleeding and never knew I got shot until Holtz told me."

Whether it was adrenaline or something else that prevented Snag from feeling the pain from being hit, that changed as soon as someone told him he'd been hit.

"It started hurting the minute Holtz told me. He's trying to bandage me, and we're taking fire. There's a sniper up in a tree, and he's trying to kill both of us now. Finally, the guys put down some fire, and I went out on my elbows dragging my leg with Edd right on me like a horse. We got behind a big anthill mound. The Doc came by and finished dressing me. Then they had to carry me damn near all day long. This happened early in the morning. And all through bomb craters, over trees, it was pretty sad because the leg was broken and I didn't want them to have to carry me. But, finally, just before dark on the last sortie, I got medevac'd out. I was done at that point."

The bullet had gone through Snag's leg, entering behind the knee, traveling through the leg and exiting several inches lower through the front of his shin. In January the previous year, he had entered the Army. Seven months into his year-long tour in Vietnam, his wound would take him to Japan, then back to the States. The war was over for Jon "Snag" Johnson.

With Snag's departure, Chris Sayre's job changed from ammo bearer to assistant gunner. He wouldn't be the assistant gunner for very long because the new machine gunner was wounded a month later. Sometime in February, Sayre began his tenure carrying the M-60 as the machine gunner.

March 1969

There was a laundry list of things to dislike as a grunt in Vietnam. Paul Decker identifies the two things he dreaded: walking point and spending the night outside the perimeter as part of the listening post (LP), an advance warning system for the rest of his platoon and company. Becoming an RTO meant he didn't have to walk point or spend a night on LP duty. As with anything, there were advantages and disadvantages of having that radio/telephone. He had the weight of that commo equipment.

Decker started out as a squad RTO, but was, at times the platoon RTO.

"I bounced back and forth between being a point RTO and the lieutenant's RTO, depending on what the needs were. Sometimes I'd be walking third behind the point man and sometimes with the lieutenant. That's how you might be rotated, at least that's how it was with me."

Although not completely certain, Decker thought it was March 7th when B2-7 nearly walked right into an NVA column.

"We were walking through the jungle, and there was kind of a clearing and a gully that went down. There was a trail we were following. The point man went down immediately, and we all went down. He looked back and he said, 'NVA.' Evidently we had walked into, on that trail, a line of NVA walking the opposite way right at us so I radioed back to the 1st platoon leader telling him what we had and he sent up Jones, who brought his M-60 with his assistant gunner. We all opened up on a mad minute on the NVA. They returned fire. I was communicating with the main CP and the mortar platoon, and I had the mortar platoon walking out mortars from our position. Fortunately, we didn't suffer any casualties that day. There was one KIA that we knew of, that we ran across this NVA body and an AK 47. That should've raised a red flag that we could be in a dangerous area if we're running into them on trails."

Decker's instincts were correct.

On the morning of March 9th, as Captain McCaffrey's RTO, Rich Dorsey was busy on the radio.

"I remember it as a huge battalion type sweep. Search and destroy. We were on the far right flank of the whole battalion on this sweep, and as our company was going through an area, I don't remember being in direct contact with other companies, but we must've been close in proximity, physically. We were going through an area. We started to walk through a clearing, hadn't run into anything. McCaffrey told Top to take a group down to our right flank even further because he said it was an area we hadn't gone through or gone over and just wanted to make sure it was clear. He didn't want to bypass it if there was anything that needed attention."

It may have been a feeling, gut instincts, but whatever it was, McCaffrey had his company looking and covering the area they were in that morning. Holtz believes that McCaffrey was sure that the company would be hit. McCaffrey wanted Holtz to take some men in one direction while the rest of company went in another direction. Different components of the company went in different directions.

"It was the 1st Platoon's turn to do a search outside of the NDP, that circle of foxholes in the jungle. We geared up, light gear, and Top came over and informed us that he was going to go on patrol with 1st Platoon. Just so happened that it was my squad, it was Beierman's squad," Decker recalls.

"I was the point radio, and Top was right in front of me. Top was right up on the point that day. There may have been one or two people in front of him. We walked through this washed out stream bed. Up that and then we came into a clearing before the jungle started again. There was maybe knee high foliage, grass, vegetation. As we were walking up, small arms fire broke out, and Top had the phone, the handset, which was obviously attached with a heavy cord to the radio on my back. It was like a crescendo of small arms fire, maybe three or four shots at first."

Jack "Squirt" Miller remembers that his group from the 1st Platoon had gone out early in the morning, had found a trail and later, around 11 a.m., crossed the creek. Climbing up out of the creek, he saw bunkers.

"They had a row of bunkers that they wanted you to see like decoys, and there was a second row of bunkers behind the first and that's where they were shooting from."

Squirt was manning the M-60.

Decker describes what followed.

"Top radioed back to McCaffrey and told him what we had. We had run into something, we weren't sure what we had in front of us. McCaffrey radioed back and said, 'Get them on line and assault'. Top looked at me and said, 'Get them on line and assault'. Top took the right side, and I took the left side. We got everybody up on line. Again, very sporadic fire, people weren't diving for cover. When the 1st Platoon was all on line, in that clearing, we were all on a line, huge line across the clearing, maybe thirty or forty of us, and we started moving forward. As we moved forward, the crescendo of firing increased, and we were firing basically from our hips as we moved closer to that jungle line—and that's when the NVA's heavy machine guns opened fire with their green tracers. When the machine guns opened up, Top was talking on the radio. He would've been on my right. Both of us dove to the ground. At the time, I was 6-2, 165 pounds, Top was probably 220. He was stocky, a solid guy, so as he dove to the right and I dove to the left, he had the radio receiver in his hand. I stopped going to the left immediately, he jerked me back with a helluva shock to the right because that's where he was going. He wasn't about to let go of the handset."

Decker continues. "From my vantage point, we could see small dark holes in the jungle, and those were the ports on their bunkers where they were firing from. We couldn't have been more than fifteen, twenty feet from that bunker complex when they opened up. Immediately, everyone went down. The grass was knee high so we had some camouflage. There were several heavy machine guns, I just know there were lots of green tracers going over. That's where I lost contact with Top. I'm not sure where he went. He could've gone to the right because he was getting everybody on line."

They were in a kill zone, and Top's priority was to get people out of the kill zone by moving toward the bunkers to eliminate the threat.

Dorsey was with McCaffrey.

"All of a sudden, from a distance, we heard some firing, a guy came on the radio and said, 'Top's been hit as well as some others, and there's a force down there that we've run into'. I told McCaffrey and his eyes got as big as saucers. That was just clear as day. He took off in a gallop towards where they were. Of course, being his radio operator, I had to stay with him for whatever he needed. I remember all that weight on my back and trying to stay up with him. I just remember running, at some point, gave out orders for support from the rest of the company to come down that way. I think there was a scattering of people in a strategic move to lend support and start to take up more of an offensive position to start to attack the enemy."

Guys went down, but the numbers of those hit and the severity of their wounds were unknown.

Though McCaffrey was on the move, the guys who had walked into the clearing and approached the jungle line with Top and Decker were still in trouble. Decker got on the radio.

"We were pinned down. I had the handset back and was talking to the main CP and the mortar platoon. The first person that came on was the FAO, who's back with the mortar platoon, and he said, 'I'm going to send some artillery marker rounds and you tell me where they drop and then we'll fire for effect'. All this time, we're firing at the bunker complex. I'd gone through all 18 clips of my M-16 so, if you were an EM [enlisted man] you weren't issued a .45, the only thing I had left was a bayonet. I remember laying there on the ground trying to dig deeper with my finger nails and the only thing I had in my hand was my bayonet. My M-16 was right next to me, but I had no rounds for it," Decker recalls.

"So, I'm on the phone and the first markers, three or four markers, when they come in they just blow up over your head, it's just smoke, no shrapnel, you tell them where that big puff of black smoke is. That smoke was right over the bunker complex, but the bunker complex was only about fifteen, twenty feet in front of us. I radioed back that, 'it was too close, you're too close, don't fire because you'll drop all that stuff on us'. Then, I hooked up with the mortar platoon on the radio, and we started walking mortar rounds in. We couldn't move. If you looked up, there was a hail of green tracers, not loud sounds, just a snapping sound when bullets are going over your head. About that time, McCaffrey came up with the main

CP to flank the bunkers in front of us."

Dorsey, with the weight of the radio, expended the effort to stay with McCaffrey as they charged toward the gunfire.

"There was a short timer, Williams, he was from Shreveport. He probably saw more stuff on the streets of Shreveport than he saw in Vietnam or at least as much. He made it very clear he wasn't going to risk his life. He had only a couple of weeks to go before his tour was up. They put him up in the CP with the idea he wouldn't go out on patrols and all and be as safe as you could possibly be and still be in the field. When McCaffrey said we're going to take this bunker out, I turned to Williams, looking him in the face. He looked at me, with the look in his eyes and simply said, 'Let's go get'em'."

"We gathered together. There was a small group of us in the CP when we finally secured what was to be our offensive actions against this enemy force because I remember us running and walking through their bunker complex with clothes still hanging on the lines. They obviously did not expect us to come. We caught them flat-footed. Whatever was hanging, it indicated that they didn't know we were in the area. We moved through a couple of bunker complexes, then gathered together at the CP, and McCaffrey said we're going to take that bunker ourselves. There was a bunker in front of us, occupied by a soldier or soldiers firing at us. And, he was determined that it was one of the key positions we had to take out. Instead of bringing others into play and telling them to go ahead, he wanted to do it.

"I remember Williams was on my left, I was in the middle, and McCaffrey was on my right as we started moving toward the bunker. We came out of a tree area and went into a little open space before the bunker, and, apparently, a machine gun opened up."

Williams was shot and killed assaulting a bunker to Dorsey's left.

"At that same moment, that machine gunner that we did not know about, not in the bunker, but off to the side in the woods, apparently did not have a clear shot at me because the bullets started coming up, almost like a trail towards me. I remember it all in slow motion. This was definitely in slow motion. I flipped out of the way. Just as I flipped, they hit my helmet with a bullet. The helmet deflected the bullet enough that it only grazed my head, blew off the helmet, and then the firing stopped. Well, it kept on for a few seconds, then stopped. It was very quiet. During that time, I played dead. I was way out in the open. I say way out in the open, but when your life is on the line, it only has to be a couple of meters to be out in the open. So, when the firing stopped, after I played dead for just a few seconds, which seemed like an eternity, all of sudden I had no idea what had happened, I got up and scrambled behind a very close tree to get cover. The medic came around the tree with McCaffrey."

Dorsey and a medic he didn't recognize were now busy with McCaffrey.

"McCaffrey's arm was shot off, at the forearm, with only skin holding it together. The medic was giving me orders to hold his arm. He showed me the position to hold the two pieces while putting on a pressure bandage. At the same time, McCaffrey starts giving orders to call in medevac, to call in support troops, to redeploy ground troops that we have. When I started to do that, it's like two people giving orders. I didn't know which order to follow. I started doing as McCaffrey ordered, but when I did that, I let McCaffrey's arm slip a bit from the position the medic wanted me to hold the arm. It was the tension between the two. But, I realized, yeah, I've got to keep the company together because this man needs some help. Then the medic and I took each side of McCaffrey and took him where he could be medevac'd out. I remember as we started to go back, all of a sudden some heads started popping up out of the bunkers that we had just been through. The medic starts yelling at me 'shoot them, shoot them'. I said, 'shoot who?' I couldn't figure out what he was talking about cause I didn't know, they were our people. He grabbed the rifle out of my hands . . . the heads went back down in the bunkers . . . and he realized they were friendlies and gave me my gun back, but he was obviously in a panic situation."

Because Holtz had been instructed to take a group of men in a different direction, he and his men had to work their way back to the firefight. By the time they reached the hot spot, what he came upon was what appeared to him as carnage. He started to help get the guys who were hit out of the hot spot.

Lt. Montgomery, listened on the radio and heard that McCaffrey had been hit.

"I told the sergeant in the mortar platoon to take charge, and I went from there by myself about 150 yards to where the company was pinned down. When I got there it was terrible. There had to be twenty or more guys on the ground, some wounded, some dead. I went over to McCaffrey, saw how bad he was hurt. McCaffrey said, 'Well, Lieutenant, you finally get what you wanted, you're the company commander'. I thought, 'This is a helluva time to promote a guy'."

B2-7 was still under heavy fire, and Montgomery needed to do something.

"NVA machine guns were still shooting, and everybody is behind anything they can get behind. Then I just got busy, took over the company, got them shooting, but they weren't shooting. There was so much incoming fire they couldn't get up to shoot so I was encouraging them. Doc Mott, the most heavily armed medic in Vietnam, he was going around and kicking guys, telling them to move. We got past that first bunker and got a perimeter started. Most of the company was spread out through some trees. Eventually, we overwhelmed the bunker with the machine gun that was doing the most damage."

Montgomery got himself positioned in front of a bunker and was yelling to get guys back into the fight. He was engaged in an exchange of hand grenades.

Squirt was fighting to take out the bunkers still firing and remembers seeing Montgomery jumping up and down, hit with grenade shrapnel.

"I was hit trying to take out a bunker. At first, I had the machine gun, handed that to Jones, then I threw a grenade at a bunker, and about the same time, the NVA threw a grenade, blowing me back. While I was on my knees, I got hit in the eyes and the bullet took out my jaw."

At some point, after being hit, Squirt remembers that someone grabbed him to find out if he was alive.

Another NVA bunker with a machine gun was taken out.

Decker was able to raise his head.

"I remember looking up. Squirt was part of the gun team, the ammo bearer on the machine gun, and he was to my right. I remember looking up over the grass as the firefight started to wind down a bit. I saw Squirt sitting on a bunker, and it didn't make sense to me because he was sitting on one of those NVA bunkers, no more than ten or fifteen feet away, and he was bobbing back and forth from the waist. And it looked like he had these huge sunglasses on, like Elton John sunglasses, but what I was seeing was where his eyes had been torn out from the round of a rifle."

Decker remembers that "somebody was yelling that we were pulling back because the firing had died down, probably after McCaffrey had flanked a few of the bunkers in front of us and where McCaffrey had been hit. I got up on my knees, kind of bent down, told to go back to the washed out creek bed. That's when I tripped over a body. I think it was Williams, obviously dead, and there was a young, stocky kid with me. He and I stopped where the body was and he looked at me and said, 'You carry him back,' and I looked at him and said, 'I've got a radio on my back, how am I going to carry him back.' So this young kid picked up the body in a fireman's carry and took him back to the washed out creek bed where everybody was gathering."

Jesse Groves saw that Williams was hit near one of the bunkers, went to him, and yelled for help to pull Williams's body back to a more secure area. Holtz saw Groves carrying Williams's body with Williams's arm draped around his neck. Holtz stepped up to take Williams's other arm.

Where possible, the wounded were being pulled out and taken to a secure area. While Pops and Holtz were carrying Williams's body to a collection point, they hit a bottleneck. Because of thick bamboo, a tunnel had to be cut under bamboo to drag bodies and the wounded through to get them to a medevac point. Squirt, following Pops and Holtz, kept walking into a wall of bamboo because his head was bandaged. Eventually, Holtz pulled Squirt down and pulled him through the bamboo tunnel. Despite the severity of Squirt's wounds, he remained conscious. After moving Williams's body, Groves and Holtz left him and returned to the firefight.

With elements of B2-7 in different places, cohesion was paramount. Montgomery was trying to pull things together where he was. Later during the firefight and after Holtz had helped with some of the wounded, Top instructed him to take over as 3rd platoon leader, normally an officer's job. Top and Montgomery seemed to be running the company together. After taking the wounded out with jungle penetrator helicopters, Top went with the rest of the company.

What Decker saw was complete chaos.

"When I got back to the creek bed, I remember the battalion was on the radio saying, 'We can't get your dead out tonight, but we can get all your wounded out, that's the priority'."

In some spots, things had wound down.

Dorsey explains that "Top gathered with us back where we were to be medevac'd. The main troops that were still in position and engaging the enemy still had more work to do, still on the front lines, reorganizing and all that."

As the day wore on and the company was able to pull back, artillery and air support was called in to blow the hell out of the bunker complex. Decker realized they had been practically muzzle to muzzle with the NVA. Based on what he heard from Battalion, he also knew that the body bags he saw would be with them on this night.

"I remember seeing the body bags waiting to be carried out the next day. That night, we basically slept with our dead."

For Dorsey, seeing McCaffrey wounded severely, he felt a rage building within him. He may have had hatred for the enemy and the desire to kill them, but after living through the firefight, the rage was aimed at "probably six to eight men in two different bunkers. I was angry because they were back behind us, they weren't up with us. I was just mad because they were playing the chicken role. They weren't up front helping us, we were alone."

B2-7 established its night defensive perimeter. The company had been shredded, mauled, losing a lot of good men. And for Holtz, though not physically injured, Top gave him a verbal scolding when he found out that Holtz had walked behind the point man after taking over as the 3rd platoon's platoon leader. Holtz didn't take it well.

"I told Top to shove it, give me back my squad."

Even in those heated moments, Top was able to take a breath and explained, "You can't walk behind the point man because you have to be a leader, and we can't afford to lose you given the state of the company after all the losses." Top didn't pull rank. He explained to Holtz why he couldn't walk second. Holtz was too valuable as a leader in the field to lose after what had happened.

It had been a horrific day. Montgomery and Top were headed to the rear. Montgomery recalled, "I waited until we got a replacement company commander out to the field. I had them set up a defensive perimeter and that's when I left the field."

Dorsey had watched his company commander medevac'd out and, despite his own wound, he was still in the field.

"There were several of us to be medevac'd, of course, taking the worst ones first. Then took the lighter wounded, including Top. He acted like he wasn't even scraped. It wasn't until he was medevac'd that I realized that he had problems, too. While we knew he was hit, yes, we thought it was worse at first, over the radio. It became clear that he wasn't as badly hurt the way he conducted himself and being among the last to be medevac'd out. I remember going back to the rear, to the medevac unit there, all of us with superficial wounds being treated. Holtz was back there and was standing over me and started laughing. I said, 'What in the world are you laughing at?' He said, 'Your head'. He thought it was like a farmer took a plow and cut a furrow through my skin to my skull and heaped the dirt up on both sides. Apparently, the bullet had come so close to the skull it bared the skull. I didn't know that."

Like a number of others, Lt. Montgomery was medevac'd at the end of the day. He needed a couple of weeks to recuperate from the grenade shrapnel.

Whether it was Dorsey, Montgomery, and Top who needed attention to less severe wounds or those like McCaffrey and Jack "Squirt" Miller who needed urgent attention to more severe and extensive wounds, the reality was that B2-7 was a changed company. A new company commander was in place the night of March 9th. In the field, the new company commander was without several key people due to wounds and the absence of Sgt. Gast who had become the company's supply sergeant at the beginning of the month.

There was a lot to do in the rear. Top, Gast, and Holtz visited the wounded and checked on McCaffrey. Gast remembered going to the morgue with Holtz to identify the dead, a task Gast had in the rear that he hated. As horrific a day as it had been, the number of soldiers killed was only three, including Williams, the short-timer, only a couple of weeks shy of making it home.

Paperwork. The Army needed to send out notifications to the families of those wounded and killed. There was a list longer than usual for March 9th, and for anyone on the receiving end, some of those notifications could seem extremely impersonal.

For the remaining able-bodied men of B2-7 still in the field, the company continued to operate in the same area for several more days. B2-7 was not the only company operating in the area because other companies in the battalion were also involved in the operation to clean out the enemy and the bunkers in the area.

The area where they had engaged the NVA was pounded daily with artillery, bombs, napalm and helicopter gunships, but that also meant that someone had to go out and assess the damage done and find out if this was resulting in enemy losses—the dreaded body count. On March 12th, the company was basically in the same area as it had been on March 9th when they had stumbled onto the NVA bunkers.

Jack Jeter, who had spent time in the rear to train as a squad leader, had become a squad leader, and Chris Sayre was now in his squad and carrying the M-60. Jeter was ordered to move his squad forward.

"My squad was on point, and I knew we were going to be ambushed so I had my guys on high alert."

Sayre recounts the obstacles and problems facing the units going out to assess the damage. The NVA were dug in well, and they would engage American units going out to assess the damage.

"Body counts were important so the day before we went, another platoon had point the day before. They were the guys who were hit and killed and whose weapons and claymores were stripped off of them by the NVA before we could get up to get their bodies back. The rest of that day, there were artillery, bombs, napalm, and helicopter gunships pounding the area. The next day, B2-7's 2nd platoon had point. We were to go up to the area of the action of the day before and cloverleaf [patrol in a cloverleaf pattern] the area. The idea was that we'd find a lot of bodies. But, the NVA were well dug in and waiting for us, having taken the claymores and blew them back on us as we approached. I didn't get hit with a claymore pellet. I may have been the thirteenth guy in line, but the first twelve did get hit. The point guy had his foot blown off. The pellets came up at an angle, hitting Jeter and our scout, a former VC, who was killed. I was back in the line. I got shrapnel later during the fight. There were twelve or thirteen people hit that day. We walked into a large NVA stronghold."

Jeter recalls that, "when I got hit, I immediately went to the ground and started returning fire. As I was changing magazines, there was the constant chatter of machine gun fire. At first I thought it was the NVA's incoming fire, and I was as flat on the ground as I could be. Then I looked to my right and noticed that the bullets going through the small brush was splintering away from me and that's when I realized it was Chris firing over my right shoulder with his M-60. I believe that if Chris hadn't been so aggressive returning fire, I would most likely be dead. After me and Barhorst drug our two most wounded guys back down the trail, Chris kept the gooks' heads down long enough for us to get the hell out of the kill zone."

Jeter, Sayre, and the rest of the squad were able to get out of the kill zone, but the cost was heavy.

Sayre notes that "we had contact every day. Eventually, they pulled us out and brought in B52s."

Between March 9th and March 13th, B2-7's company strength went from about 120 soldiers down to about 75 men. The depleted company was sent to Phuoc Vinh, the 1st Cavalry Division's base camp northeast of Saigon in order to bring it back to sufficient strength to be sent back out to fight. In the meantime, it was on "palace guard" duty as Sayre described it.

With a shrapnel wound, Sayre was another who would recuperate in country. But, Jeter's wound, while nothing like McCaffrey's or Jack Miller's, was severe enough to get him sent back to the U.S., but not severe enough to get him discharged from the army.

March 13

It was a school night, and my two younger brothers were already in bed. A friend had come by and taken my mother to get some groceries. There was an unexpected knock on the door. The taxi driver was already holding the screen door open when I opened the door. In a matter of seconds, he stuffed the envelope into my hand, turned, and was gone without a word.

It was a telegram from the Department of the Army. I knew what it was and what it wasn't. Lots of things went through my mind in an instant. Lots of emotions from fear to anger. I had to make a decision. Do I open it and read it before my mother returns or wait? I opened it, read it, digested its contents. By the time she came home, I had calmed down and understood. We would continue marking the calendar. There was school in the morning. One day at a time.

CHAPTER 8

CHANGES

J erry Gast, now in the rear as the company supply sergeant, saw more of Top after March 9th. Though Top spent time in the field, it wasn't as much as when McCaffrey was the company commander. Given the way McCaffrey had commanded the company, the odds that any new company commander would be liked as much and have men so willing to follow his lead were highly unlikely.

Gast was still adjusting to his new job as the company's supply sergeant. As a platoon sergeant, Gast saw how Top operated in the field. After March 9th, he found out, yet again, that Top did things in his own way. Supplies were not always sent by helicopter. Gast and Top would, on occasion, hook a trailer to a jeep and make a cross-country trip. Gast recounts his initial cross-country resupply trips after March 9th. The company needed to be rebuilt after the loss of so many. The supply headquarters was being moved. These trips meant taking supplies from Quan Loi to the new location, driving back and repeating the process.

"I loaded the jeep."

There was a battalion-size convoy preparing to leave and Top says, "We ain't going with them. They're going to get ambushed."

"When are we going?"

"Tomorrow," Top says.

"With who?" Gast wondered.

"By ourselves."

Gast did have some misgivings.

"You have a convoy for the whole battalion, and we're not going to go. We're going to go by ourselves, two of us. Sure enough, they were pinned down, ambushed for about four hours."

The afternoon when they decided not to go with the convoy, Top delighted in making the right decision.

"Next day, Top and I drove through there, took the same route as the convoy with a trailer full of supplies and a case of beer and our .45s. He wouldn't let me bring M-16s in case we were captured. He said, 'We're not going to give them M-16s'. We made three trips like that, and no one ever bothered us."

Chris Sayre, who went back out in the field after healing from his March 12th wound, saw differences in the company from the way it had been. He didn't see Top as much in the field. At times, the company operated in places where the people in the rear didn't want to send supplies. But, he believed that Top was fighting for them back in the rear to ensure that the guys in the field were resupplied, getting clean uniforms, and other basics.

Sayre noticed that McCaffrey's "gung-ho" approach to going out and looking for the enemy was replaced by a much more cautious approach. Sayre's impression was that the company now seemed to avoid contact and only engaged when it had to because there was no choice but to defend itself.

Attitudinal changes occurred as well. For Beierman, who had been a squad leader upon arrival in Vietnam, he had maintained a positive view of what he was doing in Vietnam.

"I think the first half of my tour I really had high hopes, my aspirations were that we're going to help this country out. The next half of the tour, I started second guessing, and we're losing men and my attitude started going to the other side that I'm going to protect my men, but anyway, that was kind of where I was sitting."

Beierman recalled that around March, perhaps after the bad days of March when the company was replacing so many men, there was an E-6 promotion board. He went before the promotion board with another guy from the company, both up to take the one E-6 slot.

"I'd been in Vietnam three months longer, and I remember going to the E-6 board. I was actually the platoon sergeant at that time, and the other guy was a squad leader. I got out of the interview, and Top looked at me and said, 'Sgt. Beierman, you have a horseshit attitude'. And, of course, he gave it to the other guy. Top had it completely right."

Holtz, who had not been wounded on March 9th, was stuck in the rear for several days. He was frustrated because he couldn't get back to the men remaining in the fight. With Top spending less time in the jungles after McCaffrey was hit, Holtz's talks with Top in the rear continued.

Several months into his year-long tour, Holtz was still grappling with the issue of fear in combat.

"I sat down with Top. I'd been through November 2nd, I'd been through January 18th with Snag. I still wasn't afraid. We started talking about fear. Top told me everybody had it, and I said I don't. It's an evolution. When I walked into the ambush on February 15th and stood and tried to walk through it again and got the shit shot out of me—and yet, not a scratch. I 'died' that night."

In fact, Holtz made it out of the ambush without a scratch but realized that he should have died.

"How do I reconcile this? I don't mind dying, but five days later, I got hit in the throat and realized, 'You may not die. They can make you bleed. They can tear you to pieces, but you may not get your wish. You may not die. You're going to have to live with what the fuck they do with you. Now go out the next day and go hunting'."

Eventually, Holtz reached the point that "I finally got to know what everybody else knows. I can't let anybody see what's going on with me. It was Top who told me. Everybody feels it, and as soon as you hear the gunfire, the fear will stop and you just go right back to work."

Lt. Montgomery, whose time in the field was significantly longer than it should have been, recuperated from his shrapnel wounds. But, he would not return to B2-7. After healing, Montgomery became the battalion liaison to the brigade.

"That meant that every afternoon at 5 o'clock, I went to a briefing and took notes. The next morning, I would get the colonel's clean uniform, get on a helicopter, fly out to where he was, present him with his uniform, start to read the notes from the meeting, and he'd say, 'Never mind I already know all that. I heard it on the radio'."

"I'd say, 'Anything else, Sir?' He'd say, 'No'. I'd go out, get on the helicopter, go back to Quan Loi, and wait until five o'clock and go to the next meeting, seven days a week. Then, I complained that I was bored."

In the Army, especially in Vietnam, complaining of boredom can have negative ramifications. The Army tried to address Montgomery's boredom.

"They made me temporary company commander of Echo Company, a recon company. I did that for a few weeks and then didn't have much to do. We'd sit around and play cards and drink beer. It could be exciting back at Quan Loi. We had nights when we'd get rocketed or mortared."

Some of the things that happened in the rear area that left memorable impressions were very different than the memorable things that happened in the field. Montgomery describes one of those impressions.

"I was in the outhouse, which was made out of ammo crates and screen. The wooden wall was about four or five feet high, but it was open air. I was in there one day and I heard a rocket coming and you can tell when they're going to hit close. It was coming close, and I was thinking, 'Geez this is a terrible way to go in a toilet'. It landed and the concussion blew me off and into the wall. My big concern was hoping no enlisted people saw this happen."

No longer in the field, B2-7 was a thing of the past for Montgomery. He still had a few months left to serve in Vietnam before getting out of the Army in August 1969, a little early so he could start college. For him, he had learned a lot from McCaffrey, who was both a leader and a teacher. Top had made a bit of an impression as well.

"TOP was a heck of soldier, incredibly disciplined and organized. We never lacked for anything."

B2-7's losses over the five days in March changed the chemistry that had existed at the top and filtered throughout the company. Because of the men lost, whether permanently or temporarily, it meant that for those remaining in the field, they had to fill important roles in the company.

Paul Decker was one of the men who remained out in the field after the wounded were medevac'd on March 9th. Decker became the RTO for the new company commander who took over B2-7. Although Dorsey had been the RTO for McCaffrey, Dorsey was in the rear recuperating from his wound, which gave Decker an opportunity to take over that position.

Dorsey returned to the field about a week after being wounded and didn't care that he was not given his old job back as the new CO's RTO.

"I believe we were in a secure area; there were huge, very deep foxholes already dug. That night, after being sent back out, our artillery started shooting. I thought it was incoming. I dove into the fox hole and landed on my head. I was so scared that it was mortars coming in, somebody said, 'Dorsey, that's our friendly fire'."

For Dorsey, things had changed dramatically.

"Frankly, I was useless after that time. I remember staying in the CP, and there was another RTO assigned to the new CO. They just had me up there where I didn't have to go on patrols if I didn't want to. I was useless. I did what I was supposed to and reacted to what I was directed, but I wasn't proactive like I was with McCaffrey. It just messed me up."

For Decker, he stayed out in the field until he suffered through a series of incidents that may have earned him a safer job. Being the company RTO, he had gotten familiar with what was supposed to happen in the field.

"Infantry companies had a procedure that when you are traveling through the jungle on a search and destroy mission, that your sister companies would mortar your old position. We knew that after we left an NDP and got six or seven klicks away, our sister company would mortar the old position in the hope of catching the NVA there scavenging for anything we may have left behind. The NVA would look for food or ammunition or anything else that might be useful too them. Basically, we had the grid zeroed in so that at a prescribed time our sister company would mortar the old NDP after we'd moved out.

"One particular night, for some reason, our sister company never received a message that we weren't moving. We were going to stay in our NDP for another day and another night. About midnight, one o'clock, mortars started raining down on us. I don't know if it was friendly fire or

NVA. In any case, we had built a bunker with sandbags, bamboo on top of that and then more sand bags. A blast went off behind me, lifted me up, and threw me into this bunker. The large bamboo poles rammed the lower left quadrant of my abdomen. It was painful at the time, but I didn't think much of it. It didn't break the skin. It was just a blunt injury.

"The next day, I was in a lot of pain. One of our medics, he looked and said, 'Don't worry about it. It's just one of your glands developing'. That night, I just couldn't go on any farther. We went to another LZ, I was back with 1st Platoon as the RTO and I was spiking a temperature, sicker than a dog. They took me over to the medical bunker at this LZ. One of the medics looked and said 'You're swollen, it's a hernia'. They medevac'd me to a hospital.

"I found out that it was an infected abdominal hematoma, about the size of a tennis ball. A large pocket of infection developed where the blunt trauma had occurred. I spent nine days in the hospital. Then, when I was discharged from the hospital, I went back to Quan Loi. I met with Top and Gast back at B Company. I showed them the papers that said I was on light duty for a week.

"Gast said, 'B Company was real light. The company is out on LZ Jamie. We're going to send you out to LZ Jamie, a forward LZ, and you can remain there until you are no longer on light duty'. I went out to the helipad and was flown to LZ Jamie. I got to the LZ and reported to the CO. The CO said, 'The company is moving off the LZ today. You have a choice. You can stay on the LZ or move out with us.' I told him that I was on light duty. On the LZ, there was hot food, artillery, and hot showers. The CO said to another captain to take care of me.

"I was assigned to a front-line bunker on the LZ. A couple of nights later, about one o'clock in the morning, we were hit hard by maybe a regiment of NVA. They blew the concertina wire in front of us, and they took over five or six bunkers. They were inside the wire. They were running around the LZ shooting people. We fought till about six in the morning. There were just piles of bodies. The NVA had taken over and killed the GIs in the front bunkers on the other side of the perimeter from where I was. In the morning, some of the NVA were still in or on the bunkers they'd overrun. So, some howitzers were rolled toward the bunkers that the NVA had, and howitzers were used point blank to eliminate those bunkers with the NVA."

Decker was busy surviving the NVA's attack from his bunker position. The Army's after action report indicated that a mortar barrage was how the attack on LZ Jamie began. The NVA waited for the mortars and rocket-propelled grenades to get the Americans hunkered down before they attacked and made attempts to penetrate the perimeter, using satchel charges. The NVA blew the wire and made it into the perimeter and into several bunkers that had been manned by the Americans. The NVA were engaged by the men on the LZ but also engaged by gunships and air support. There was a lull a couple of hours after it had started, but the NVA was not finished as another barrage of the LZ began, which was shorter than the initial barrage. By dawn, the battle was over but had required fire support from another nearby LZ, as well as the air strikes and gunships. Nearly fifty Americans were killed and wounded. Over fifty NVA were killed inside the perimeter.

"During the night, that area where I had been injured and had been treated, started to swell again. In the morning, it was chaos. We had some killed, and there may have been about 170 NVA killed inside and outside of the perimeter. I went to the med tent and explained that I had reinjured my abdomen. They sent me back to Quan Loi, an aide station there, and I got another week of light duty and then reported back to B Company.

"Back at B Company, Top and Gast were running the company from Quan Loi."

Decker recalls that the Army decided to provide him with a unique opportunity.

"Gast said there was an officer who wanted to meet with me. This officer said he was a recruiter. He said he noticed I had passed the warrant flight test. He said, 'Based on the information I have here, I guarantee you that if you re-up for another three years, starting right now, we'll get you out of here and send you to pre-flight'. After six months in the bush with Bravo Company, I'd had enough Army up to my neck. I graciously declined."

Flying for the Army in any capacity was no longer of interest to Decker.

"Top sent me out to the Green Line at Quan Loi. Quan Loi is a huge LZ, more secure than being out in the jungle. There was an airstrip on Quan Loi. It wasn't bad duty, unless you're being rocketed. I was assigned to this bunker for guard duty. About the second day, I was covered in mud because of the rain and being in a dirt bunker. A jeep pulled up with Gast in the passenger seat. I got out of the bunker and walked toward the jeep and Gast says, 'You want a rear job?' I turned around to look behind me to see who he was talking to. Gast says, 'I'm talking to you'. I said, sure. 'They're looking for an E-5 or a damn good E-4'."

Decker went back to the B Company area to get showered and to put on a clean uniform so he could be interviewed by a colonel for the job in the rear. The job was split between a civilian personnel office and a medical battalion in Quan Loi. Decker's interview went well. He was done with the infantry and had a new job. He was transferred out of B2-7. When Decker thanked Gast, Gast said, "Don't thank me, thank Top."

It was June 1969, and Decker was done as an infrantryman. Around the same time, Skinny got his buck sergeant stripes and also got pulled back to a rear job. Skinny had done a lot of walking point and had survived.

From time to time, Top got jobs for his grunts so that they could get out of the jungles. As a First Sergeant, he likely heard the scuttlebutt in the rear about personnel needs either from other senior NCOs or officers within the battalion above the company level.

CHAPTER 9

TIME SERVED

Men arrived in Vietnam with no fanfare, and they left that way. Replacements had been assigned to B2-7 in ones and twos, and they left either because they made it through their year-long tour or because they had been wounded or killed. For those who were lost to wounds or killed in action, there was little or no time for the survivors to grieve. The survivors remained in the field, continued to fight, and needed to clear their heads so that they could continue functioning and keeping each other alive.

For Jon "Snag" Johnson, after being wounded on January 18th, he remained in the Army for seven more months, spending six months at an Army hospital. Snag spent seven months and twenty-two days in Vietnam. But, his time in the company with Top had been only about a month and a half and with Captain McCaffrey a month longer.

It was just eight days before his 21st birthday when Jack Miller was wounded by a grenade and blinded by a bullet. While Holtz and others helped him to a collection point for the wounded, Jack "Squirt" Miller remembered that Top was with him for a few minutes before being medevac'd out on March 9th. Between the time Decker and Top were separated and McCaffrey was hit, Top had fought through NVA bunkers and found the collection point for the wounded. Squirt remembered Top leaving him when word came that McCaffrey was wounded. Squirt was medically attended to for an extended period of time and was discharged from the Army in June 1969. Since the day he was hit, his body has yielded over 300 pieces of shrapnel, and, to this day, he still feels pieces of grenade shrapnel making their way through his body.

Jack Jeter's leg wound, five and a half months into his tour of duty, got him out of Vietnam. Over several weeks, he was transferred from one medical facility to another. Starting with his initial treatment in Vietnam, he was sent to Japan for a couple of weeks before being flown to the U.S. and, eventually, to Brooke Army Hospital at Ft. Sam Houston, Texas. At Brooke Army Hospital, it was so full of wounded that there wasn't room for all the patients so some were simply in the hospital's hallway. Jeter remained in the hospital until sometime in June 1969.

Around July 10, 1969, Jeter was notified and instructed to report to Ft. Hood. Because of his leg wound, he also had a medical profile that documented his problems in stooping, bending, running, and other physical limitations. The medical profile prevented him from certain forms of duty and physical activities for the remainder of his time in the Army.

"Some kid checking me in said, 'I see you were wounded in combat. Well, because of that you have a choice, do you want to be in infantry or armor?' I said, 'Fuck infantry, I want to be in armor'. They put me in a tank battalion. They sent me over to a company, and because I was a sergeant, they gave me a room."

"The first morning I was there, after reveille, the first sergeant comes out and asks me, 'Sgt. Jeter, have you ever been in tanks before?' I said, 'No, First Sergeant, I haven't'. He gives me a stack of books and says, 'Here, study these. You're now a tank commander'. So, within about three or four weeks, I was teaching classes. I was a tank commander from July '69 until May 12, 1970. But I was never there. I'd just leave, go out to the lake, go swimming, drink beer, and hang out with the guys. I'd show up for reveille and head count in the evening. I'd go to the motor pool a few days a week and work on the tank, and usually, I'd climb in the driver's seat, lock the hatch and go to sleep. That's what I did for most of the last eight or ten months."

Having already been in Vietnam, having seen what he'd seen and having been through firefights and, at times, not knowing if he and or his buddies would make it out of life and death situations, dealing with soldiers or officers who had not been to Vietnam did not always bring out the best of Jeter, but he was able to display a sense of humor.

"We had this second lieutenant who thought he was hot shit in our company. I'd be walking through the motor pool, and we had the baseball hat type of caps, so when I'd see him coming, I'd throw my right hand up to the bill of my cap like I was going to salute, but just remove the hat and wipe my forehead. I used to fuck with that guy unmercifully. He hated me because he wasn't getting the respect he thought he should get.

"I carried that medical profile with me. One time, I was watching my guys wash a tank and was just standing there when that second lieutenant says, 'You realize there's mud underneath that tank?', and I said, 'No, Sir, I sure didn't'. The lieutenant says, 'You bend over and take a look at it'. I said, 'No, Sir, can't do it'. I pull that medical profile and show it to him, and he'd get furious.

"Then, one day in May, one morning, it was all over. Really anti-climactic getting out. That was a fast two years. I survived, unbelievable. I really love the guys I served with, but as far as the Army, what a joke, there's so much bullshit."

A few years later, it hit home for Jeter.

"I went back to riding dirt bikes within six months of getting out of the Army. I remember in '75 when I was really riding hard and winning, one day I was getting ready to practice and putting on my riding gear. I was walking through the living room, and I saw the evacuation of the Embassy in Saigon. I felt like crying, what a goddamn waste."

For those who made it to the end of their tour of duty, there was a magic day when it was time to start processing out of Vietnam. Jesse Groves made it through his year-long tour. He'd become a squad leader well into his year and completed his twelve months without being wounded, although a lot of guys around him were wounded.

"The good NCOs we had like Holtz and Gast helped save lives. A lot of guys are alive because of the leadership we had. Top's the type that fits the 'hero' meaning. Some want to do just enough to get by. Top wasn't like that. If anybody ought to have been a Sergeant Major, he should've been, but probably he was too honest. He'll tell you he doesn't agree if you say something."

Top left different impressions on Pops. There were things that Top did in the field that had left impressions, but there were also impressions because of moments in the rear. In addition to leaving Vietnam without being wounded, he gave up drinking whiskey and coke mixed drinks and decided to stick with beer. Top was serious and all business in the field and he was equally good at relieving stress in the rear.

"Top let go . . . that's the way he was, relieving the stress, having drinks with the guys . . . he stood out. I was with Holtz and Top at a bar in the rear area, drinking coke and whiskey . . . got dry heaves from the drinking so I blame Top for not wanting to drink coke and whiskey ever again. I drank a lot of beer after that."

Pops was in the field until about a week before it was time to leave Vietnam. There was no "transition" other than time to process out. By mid-April 1969, Pops was stateside to finish out the last six months of his time in the Army. Having spent a year as an infantryman, it made sense to someone somewhere, probably in the bowels of the Pentagon, for Pops to be assigned to a mechanized unit at Ft. Meade, Maryland.

"I saw tanks only twice the whole time in Vietnam," Pops recalled.

Time was filled practicing riot control in case his unit was called out during a riot. At the other end of the spectrum, the unit practiced for parades. No matter what it was, it was better than Vietnam.

Pops' bottom line about it all was that "all in all it was a good experience, but if you asked me to do it again, No. I would never have volunteered for it. It changed my life. You get perspective about what it means, what somebody pays, the cost of defending the country, and what it feels like to have your life totally changed."

In the end, Vietnam was the same for him as it was with practically anyone serving on the front lines of the fight.

"My job as a squad leader was to keep guys alive and ensure that we got home alive. We had to look after each other." While the bonds created with some of the guys in his squad and his platoon became strong during his tour of duty, Pops knew that "the Army wasn't going to be my life. I'd rather drive a garbage truck."

When it was time, he returned to civilian life.

Beierman and Holtz, who had arrived in Vietnam about a month apart in August and September 1968, were headed home in early June 1969. Both received early-outs because they had been accepted at different schools.

Beierman, whose father had been a World War II veteran, had arrived in Vietnam with what might be viewed as some naïve thoughts of what was doable, but that had changed during his tour of duty. As Top had recognized, his attitude had changed.

"I think my attitude, because of what was going on, I think we all had it, we just got a little sullen. I'm thinking I'm not sure that what we're doing here is going to accomplish anything."

That change in attitude, however, did not diminish his commitment to keep his men safe and alive.

Before leaving Vietnam, the CO who had replaced McCaffrey had one last "favor" he wanted from Edd Holtz. Holtz had been out of the field for a week or so.

"I went out to say goodbye to everybody. I'd been running a platoon so I just went back to where the platoon was set up and sat down next to the radio. Carter calls my radio operator and he says, 'Tell Holtz to saddle up a squad. He's going to go out on patrol'. I told the radio operator to tell Carter to go straight to hell. Holtz wasn't going anyplace. Carter's back on the horn and says, 'Let me talk to Holtz'. He told me that the CO wanted me to saddle up a squad and take them out on patrol. I told him, 'the CO can tell me to go to hell. I wasn't going anyplace. I was here to say good-bye. I'm going home tomorrow'. Next thing I know, the CO is on the horn. The CO says, 'I'll brew up a cup of cocoa, come on up here. Let's talk'. I'd spent months with this guy. I knew the CO real well. He knew me real well. When he needed something real bad, he'd come to me, and we'd work it out. He said, 'You've been gone and we've run into gooks, nobody has fired their rifle, we'd been shot up and have nothing to show for it. We passed a 500-pound bomb coming in here today, and I'm going to go out there and blow it whether you take me or not. But, I'd sure feel better if you'd take me'. So, I went back, hand-picked a squad. I walked point going out, and I walked drag coming back. And I was never so afraid in my life. Ever. I finally got to know what everybody else knows."

Holtz made it to the end of his tour of duty, to a large extent because earlier TOP and McCaffrey had made sense to him about what needed to be done. To Holtz, McCaffrey, Top, and Gast had been the keys to pulling it off from a leadership perspective and the support of the machine gunners —all the pillars that made it all work and allowed Holtz to do what he had done. Otherwise, he believed he wouldn't have made it. He had served with incredible individuals like Snag Johnson, who was willing to run into gunfire.

"You won't find a Top or McCaffrey or Gast when you need them in the right spot, that combination and that's what made us successful. We needed Top and McCaffrey for what they gave us. They gave us the 'finishing school'."

The experience gained during that tandem of leadership carried him through under a new CO and till the end of his tour.

Holtz left Vietnam and was discharged from the Army in early June 1969 and was sitting in a university classroom by mid-month. In a period of six days, he went from the jungles of Vietnam to a classroom in Illinois.

Was Vietnam supposed to be locked away as if it had never happened?

Jerry Gast and Rich Dorsey were headed home in July 1969. Upon landing in the U.S., Dorsey felt an immediate difference. When he was in B2-7, there had been a sense of being cared for, but it was a two-way street. Everyone looked out for each other. Thinking about Top, "You knew he cared. There was never a doubt in my mind that by following him, he would always have my back."

In the airport terminal, upon arriving in California, "I was expecting people to greet us. There wasn't anybody. I got in the terminal. I was walking down the terminal, in my uniform. I distinctly remember people walking towards me, about to come by me, and they would go over to the other side of the hall to get as far away as possible to go by me in the opposite direction. I didn't know fully, of course, being out in the field not getting the news that much, what the sentiment was against the war and, not only against the war, but the soldiers."

Dorsey was not aware of the impact that the My Lai massacre had had on the general public. The actions of a handful of GIs had led to the way many Americans painted all the Vietnam veterans as war mongers, slaughtering innocent civilians.

"I was treated like crap. Even during the thirty-day leave, my immediate family was trying to be sensitive to me. I realized there was a distinct feeling out there when I'd be out in public in civilian clothes, people who knew I had been in Vietnam, treated me differently. It's just continued to hurt very deeply."

After his 30-day leave, Dorsey headed to D.C. to finish his last six months in the Army. When he reported for duty, he was told, "We're going to have you in the Honor Guard." It would be a lot of spit and polish to be in the Honor Guard.

"I sat down and someone put something in front of me to sign and said, 'Here, you have to sign up for this. The training alone is six months so you have to re-up for two years'. I said, 'No way. Thanks, but no thanks. I've had enough of this man's army'." By refusing to re-enlist, Dorsey was transferred to Ft. Campbell, Kentucky. He spent the last six months assisting a drill instructor in pushing trainees through basic training. Given the dire situation the Army was in by mid-1969, Dorsey likely saved himself from a second tour of duty in Vietnam by refusing to sign that piece of paper. The Army would have loved having an experienced junior NCO back in Southeast Asia.

Gast left Vietnam a few weeks short of a year. Except for Top's interactions with McCaffrey, Jerry Gast may have been the next person within B2-7 with whom Top interacted the most. Because Gast had been a platoon sergeant when Top arrived, which meant interaction with Top, and as the supply sergeant in the rear, Gast worked with Top regularly. From the initial days when Gast had been shocked to see a first sergeant in the field till the end of his tour of duty in Vietnam, everything about the way he thought of this first sergeant had changed. He had seen how Top put experience to work, what Top expected in the field and how Top interacted with guys in the rear. As time passed, Gast's trust in Top's instincts were complete.

"I always believed from dealings that I had in the field with Top, even out of the field, what he told you he wanted to do was because that's what's going to keep you alive. He was a professional, experienced combat soldier. He had no fear. He may have had the fear but never showed it."

Toward the end of July, Top also took a "break" from Vietnam. On the evening of the moon landing in July 1969, Top arrived at home for a month's leave. One of the factors that played into his desire to go home was the birth of another son who had been born in June. But, by taking the month-long break, it meant that when he went back to Vietnam in August, the end of his tour of duty would not end a month later than it would have, but would be sometime in early 1970. That, however, did not play out as intended. In January 1970, Top was burned badly enough to be medevac'd and sent to Japan for treatment for his burns. It was the last time he left Vietnam. After his burns had been treated in Japan, Top headed back to the U.S. He moved his family from California back to Ft. Knox, Kentucky.

Paul Decker, who had transferred out of B2-7 in May 1969, extended his tour of duty in Vietnam by two months in order to avoid stateside duty. He was discharged from the Army after nineteen months of service, though he had spent fourteen of those months in Vietnam.

Chris Sayre served under three company commanders, starting with McCaffrey. By the time he was serving under his third captain, he had noticed a very distinct drop in quality. He made it to the end of his year-long tour in Vietnam and still had half a year remaining. Like some before him, he learned that the Army does things without any of it making any sense.

Sayre headed to Ft. Hood, Texas.

"They offered a promotion as an incentive to re-enlist. There was no way an offer could be attractive enough to stay in the Army." Sayre did not care about becoming a sergeant. At Ft. Hood, he was assigned to an artillery group, Honest John rockets. "It was a whole different world from being in the infantry. It was strange coming back."

Coming back and serving stateside was strange in other ways as well. Stateside duty meant putting up with menial bullshit. In Vietnam, as a combat soldier, Sayre learned what was important relating to survival and protecting his buddies. He found out that simply having a moustache attracted unwanted attention at Ft. Hood. Sayre never suspected that there could be a problem because his first sergeant, whose name was Peppers, at Ft. Hood, had a Beatles album cover framed behind his desk.

Sayre remembers that the first sergeant took one look at him and said, "I don't like moustaches."

Sayre thought he could reason with the first sergeant saying, "Well, First Sergeant, as long as I keep it trimmed and within regulations, I have a right to keep it."

The first sergeant just smiled.

"The next thing I know, my name is on every shit duty you can think of . . . KP, CQ, runner, guard duty, whatever. So, I shaved the moustache off, and then when he saw me, he smiled and took my name off of all the lists. I had about two weeks left in the Army so I started growing it back and as soon as he saw the shadow again, my name got back on the lists."

In June 1970, Sayre was discharged. He grew the moustache back and has had it ever since. Given the times and the hostility toward Vietnam veterans, he grew a full beard and let his hair grow long. The negativity caused him to put everything related to Vietnam in a box and put it all away in the basement.

CHAPTER 10

LIFE MARCHES ON

Around late February or March 1970, Top and family drove cross country back to a familiar post, Ft. Knox. Generally, life at Ft. Knox was not that different in 1970 from what it had been 1966. First Sergeant Trainer was back at a basic training company where recruits were going through that ordeal.

Ft. Knox High School was across the road, within easy eye-sight of the elementary school that I had left in 1966. Given the country's mood toward Vietnam, living on post was a good thing. The contrast between what was going on in civilian communities and on post was interesting, to say the least, when it came to high school students.

While civilian kids were wearing Army fatigue shirts and jackets and placing interesting non-military patches on them, Ft. Knox High School students were not wearing them, at least not to school. There was no tolerance for students wearing any items of an Army uniform. Ft. Knox High School students were also adhering to a very strict hair length code, well, especially for the boys. In 1970 and 1971, the High School's principal was intimidating. He had been a basketball player in Kentucky and towered over everyone. It was not uncommon for him to wander through every home room in the mornings and check on dress and hair code adherence.

At some point, the son of the Post's commanding general found the rules to be a bit much for his liking and decided the local civilian high school might be more to his liking. His experiment lasted, possibly, two days before he was back at Ft. Knox High School. If there was anyone who was expected to follow the rules, he was that person.

Ft. Knox was our last posting. Upon reporting in for duty at Ft. Knox, First Sergeant Trainer learned that he would be back on orders to return to Vietnam, despite the fact that he'd just returned from Vietnam and had just moved his family cross-country. He submitted his papers to retire. In February 1971, Top retired with over twenty-one years on active duty.

Fred Hall and the young men of B2-7 were either drafted or saw the writing on the wall and "volunteered." By the time most were discharged from the Army, they were still in their mid and early 20s. Barry McCaffrey, after a prolonged period of medical attention and rehabilitation, remained in the Army, taught at West Point, and then moved on to other assignments.

At some point after retiring, Top had an urge to try and locate McCaffrey. After some cajoling of someone at the Pentagon, Top was able to extract McCaffrey's contact information from some reluctant duty officer. That allowed him to eventually trek to West Point for the two to reconnect.

Life marched on. Jobs, marriages, children were the focal points for everyone during the intervening years. But, it was impossible to forget that time in their lives when they lived primitively. They were together 24/7. It was an intimate existence. They experienced the rawest and most intense human emotions, living on the edge of life and surviving. They experienced it together. Among themselves, there was no need to explain anything.

Pops had said that it had been a challenge adapting to the Army when he was inducted. It was no different getting out.

"It's not normal for a person to go through this experience and be normal ever again. It's not normal to go out and possibly be killed or look to go out to kill others".

Pops moved on. The negativity toward Vietnam veterans affected him from the perspective of not wanting to talk about that period of his life. Being back in the States, he equated his feeling like that of a convict because of the treatment and the way Vietnam veterans were characterized.

To some extent, this was not very different than how Dorsey felt when he finally recognized the negative reactions of people at the airport when he landed in California.

Jack Jeter was back in Texas, had a successful business, and despite a bad knee from his wound, eagerly returned to cross-country dirt bike riding. But, he also had an urge to see the guys he had served with in Vietnam. His first attempt was a drive from Texas to Virginia to see his former squad leader. After a day or two, it became apparent that his desire to meet was not met with the same level of interest, or perhaps, it was far too soon to revisit Vietnam. Jeter drove back to Texas.

Although there was no internet, several guys tracked each other down. They were scattered around the country, but Jeter remembers getting together with Holtz, Skinny, Sayre, and a couple of other guys in either 1982 or 1983. Sayre believes that it was '83. More than a decade after Vietnam, Jeter remembers that "we were all skinny and had hair".

Sayre remembers getting a call in 1983. He thinks it was Holtz.

"This guy starts asking me all these questions, and I'm thinking who the hell is this guy. It was Holtz. Holtz, Jeter, Skinny, myself, and two others, we converged on Chicago for a weekend. Holtz got rid of his family. We went to Edd's house and just reliving what we've done in the last thirteen years and going back to all the stuff from Vietnam."

The desire to locate and get back together with others from B2-7 grew.

"The second reunion in 1985, the guy who took McCaffrey's place in Vietnam, came to that reunion and helped us get in contact with McCaffrey. That's how we started putting the company back together," Sayre explained.

It wasn't until 1987 that Jeter finally experienced anything like appreciation for his service in Vietnam. And, of course, it was on an Army post. He and a few others headed to Ft. Benning, Georgia, for a reunion of a small group of B2-7 guys with McCaffrey, who was by then wearing stars on his shoulder.

"It was a helluva trip to Ft. Benning. That was the first time I saw Top after Vietnam. Me and Chris Sayre and Skinny and Eckel, we all got there about the same time and rented a Lincoln Continental and went from Atlanta to Ft. Benning and drinking Tequila the whole time. We were really screwed up by the time we arrived on post."

McCaffrey had arranged for the guys to stay in Bachelor Officer's Quarters. Sayre described some of what occurred the next day.

"McCaffrey meets us, and we spent the day reviewing troops. We went out to a live fire exercise and watched these kids going through all the stuff. McCaffrey took us to one of the mess halls for lunch where the cattle trucks are driving up and the drill sergeants are barking at these kids, making them get down and do pushups. It was like reliving life for us from years earlier. Then, he asked us what else would we like to do, and I wanted to fire an M-60 so he took us to a range. They had a couple of M-60s set up with a couple of boxes of ammo, and I got to fire an M-60 again."

The other activity occurring on post that day was a combined graduation ceremony for those completing basic training and AIT. That meant that there were a lot of families attending and a lot of troops on a parade ground.

"We drive up. The troops are on the parade field. Families are in the bleachers. McCaffrey had told them not to wait for him, but they did and these families are there, it's hot. He was not happy. We go walking in, we sit down. He grabs the microphone and apologizes to the families and the troops. And says, 'There's a special reason why I'm late.' He introduces us. He explained that we are the guys he was with in Vietnam. That was our welcome home," Sayre recalls.

"That was the very first time as a Vietnam Veteran that I thought we got any recognition," Jeter remembers. "Everybody in the stands got up and applauded."

Perhaps with time, it became easier for some to reconnect. In any case, Jeter and others worked to find more of the guys. The internet helped. As those efforts were underway, Top stayed in touch with McCaffrey and was invited to the Pentagon for McCaffrey's retirement from the Army in 1996.

Like the way guys arrived and left B2-7 in Vietnam, it was the same in tracking people down. It was a bit of a slog, tracking people down one by one. One of the challenges was to remember someone's real name. Once people got used to using someone's nickname, a real name may have been forgotten.

"Snag," who was that? What's his real name? Oh, in Snag's case, "Jon" isn't spelled the way one would naturally spell it, yet another complicating factor.

"Squirt?"

Slowly, the names were figured out and the search undertaken. By the late '90s, there was a sufficient number who had been tracked down, and there were reunions held in the Washington, D.C., area coinciding with Veteran's Day or Memorial Day.

After Lt. Montgomery left B2-7 for the job in the rear as the liaison officer, he had occasion to socialize with Top, who was spending a little less time in the field after McCaffrey was wounded. But, after leaving the Army, it was decades before the two would meet again. Gast and Jeter were able to locate Montgomery. Montgomery believes it was 1997 when he saw Top for the first time after Vietnam. It was a chance to continue socializing. But, Montgomery's trip to D.C. hadn't been without its problems.

Montgomery explains.

"First time I saw Top again, after all those years, was when I first went to Washington. I had taken a red eye out of Nevada. I got there at seven in the morning. My bags were lost. I was beat, and I didn't sleep all night. I got to my room, took a shower, and tried to get the airlines to help me get my bags. I laid down about noon to take a nap, and a few minutes later, the phone rings. It was the 1st Sergeant and he says, 'Lieutenant, you want to come down and have a drink with your old First Sergeant?' I'm not going to let him know I'm tired, so I said, 'Absolutely.' I was beat. I got up and went down there. It was about one o'clock in the afternoon when I got down there and at two in the morning, we were still down there. I had quit several times. It was getting ridiculous, and he was still going strong." Montgomery doesn't remember when he stumbled off to bed.

"The next morning at six o'clock, the phone rings, and it was McCaffrey and I found myself saying, 'Yes, sir?'"

Despite the many years, some things never changed.

Jack "Squirt" Miller remembers getting a call from one of the B2-7 guys and being encouraged to call Top. He was reluctant. He really hadn't had much direct contact with Top in Vietnam. Squirt hadn't been a platoon sergeant or a squad leader. In fact, he had arrived in Vietnam and been with the company about the same length of time as McCaffrey. About the only concrete thing he remembered was Top sitting with him before being medevac'd on March 9, 1969.

"It was thirty years later, and I wondered why I would call him. He wouldn't remember me. Anyway, I called. Top answered the phone, and I asked him, 'What were you doing on March 9, 1969?' He said, 'I was in a firefight'. Then, I asked him, 'Do you remember a guy called Squirt?' Top says, 'Jack Miller'. I couldn't believe he remembered my name."

Pops was initially contacted by Holtz. Looking back, Pops admits that they may not have been friends if they had simply met in civilian life. They were very different. But, in Vietnam, because of circumstances, they clicked and got along very well. Pops is a regular attendee now at "Camp Gast" in the summers. He knows it took all of them together to get through Vietnam, but despite understanding that, when it came to Top, it was simple.

"I thought the world of him. Still do."

Fred Hall's life had marched on as well, but in a wholly different way. His links to Top had ended around September or October 1968 when Top left his basic training company at Ft. Ord in order to prepare for Vietnam. Hall had been discharged in early 1969. Hall didn't give much thought to the Army or Top. He did, occasionally, think about a few of the recruits he had been given only because a few had become successful athletes or entertainers.

In 2002, Hall was retiring from his job as the director, Palatine, Illinois Park District. His colleague and successor was tabbed to help with a "surprise" retirement party.

"Ron, who had worked for me for twenty-five years came to me and said he needed a list for the party. I gave him a list of names, including the names of anybody who bought me a beer so it was a long list."

After he looked over the list, Ron returned. He says, "A name's missing: Top."

After hesitating a moment, I said, "I haven't seen Top since '68." That's when Ron pointed something out. He said, "Do you know how often, how much you mention him? You always mention that 'this is how Top would do this or that'."

The reality was that Hall had not been conscious of it. He had no idea how often he had mentioned Top over the years. It was Ron who noticed. Fred had adopted a number of things, the way Top did things. Fred had adopted the way Top conducted staff meetings. Hall remembered that when staff meetings ran long, the next meeting would be conducted standing up, no chairs, no ashtrays, nothing available that might drag a meeting on endlessly. Hall recalled that, "Meetings in the day room could go on a long time. So, the next time we had a meeting in the day room, Top would make sure that there was no coffee or ashtrays to get it moving."

It had been thirty-four years. With the help of a friend and the internet, the hunt began. Eventually, the hunt paid off, and, in the end, Top wasn't all that far away. Top attended Hall's retirement party. At the time of Hall's retirement and roughly sixty years of life, Top had only been a part of it for nine months. Hall reflected on Top's influence on him.

"He has something special. A gift to train people and to lead people. He can be gentle and the biggest pain in the ass. He's got the gift for bringing out the best in somebody and knows when to prod or cajole as well as knowing when to give a kick in the ass. His timing was always excellent."

Though Hall had been Top's subordinate, Hall's outreach to Top renewed their friendship. And, through Top, Hall met the men of B2-7. Over the past decade, Hall has attended the reunions and the summer gatherings at Camp Gast. His observations of Top, when he was a young DI, have been re-enforced and broadened.

"My opinions of Top aren't the result of a bulb going off, but a collection of these impressions formed when in my 20s, re-enforced as I got older."

Even now, as those once young B2-7 soldiers near seventy, some already there, Hall observed.

"I see how he still commands the respect that he earned in Vietnam with people who he had to yell at, berate in order to keep them alive. There are lots of different personalities among the men, but it all comes back to the same thing. Everybody loves and respects him. They don't want to cross him. They all, we all, recognize the tone of voice or the look, Top's eyes."

"I saw him in a totally different light. I was a garrison soldier and the rest of the guys got to know him and respect his leadership, his care, and that's what drives him. He'd never want me to say that, 'Top is a very caring person'. I'd get that look. But he is," Hall said as he reflected.

"We've all had people whose first thought in an employer-employee relationship is, 'I've got to cover my ass,' and we've all, hopefully, all of us have been fortunate enough to work for somebody who says, 'I'll cover my subordinate's ass, then I'll worry about my own.' Top, in my opinion, was always more concerned about covering my ass than his own."

Hall also recalled Top's respect for rank.

"Top chewed my ass when he heard me call one of our lieutenants some derogatory term. He got all over me. He called the lieutenant in and said, 'Sgt. Hall has something to say to you'. He didn't tell me what I had to say, I just knew it. I had to apologize to him. I owed it to the rank. He respected rank. We had a CO who Top despised, but he'd still give him the same snap salute, the same respect. We all knew he was respecting the rank, not the person."

Hall compared his first sergeant in AIT to Top.

"One big difference and I don't think I knew it until I met Top. The difference was that my AIT first sergeant, although he was a good NCO, he worked a lot harder for the people above him than he did for the people who worked for him."

Hall, based upon his own experiences and listening to the guys of B2-7 around the campfire, reached his conclusions.

"When the guys around the camp fire talk about how they're surprised when they turn around, after having worked for other first sergeants in Vietnam, they turn around and here's Top walking about four feet behind point with a double-bladed ax because he couldn't see well enough to shoot a rifle. You don't learn that. Some of the best skills in life are caught, they aren't taught. Top caught these things. He has the 'something,' the 'it' that very few people have. He leads by walking into a room. He doesn't need anybody to say, 'good job'. He just doesn't need much other than what's inside him. He's at peace with himself because he knows where he is, what he is."

CHAPTER 11

RECOGNITION

M ost of B2-7's young soldiers who were drafted or volunteered for the draft fulfilled their military obligations before they had their own families. For most, it was a chapter of their lives that was started and completed before there were any spouses or children. They packed it away, and it may not have been necessary to revisit and relive that part of their lives after they had their own families. The Army chapter that included their tour of duty was finished and locked away for some. Locking it away and hoping to keep it that way wouldn't be so surprising given the overall public opinion and attitudes toward the men who fought in Vietnam.

Upon discharge, they returned to civilian life and went to school, got jobs and started families and businesses. It is safe to say that for most of the spouses and probably all of the children, the Army was past history, not their reality. Except for a very few, their spouses and children never saw them in uniform and, perhaps, never saw pictures of them in uniform. Or, maybe family members saw pictures of them only in the worn-out fatigues worn in the jungles, but not the dress uniforms with their ribbons. There may have been passing references to having been in the Army, something not worth dwelling on for the benefit of children unborn at the time.

Men who have been in war, especially those who fought in an unpopular war, may be very reluctant to talk about it except with their brothers in arms. At B2-7 reunions, the men who were just teenagers or barely into their twenties in Vietnam are now sometimes accompanied by their adult children, born after their dads were in the Army. The level of their knowledge of what their fathers went through ranges dramatically from a lot to practically nothing.

In many ways, these adult children of many B2-7 soldiers may be more like my youngest brother, born after my father retired from the Army, having never been an army brat and never having experienced the war in any way. Spared, if you will, of the concerns that accompany that type of life.

Returning to the question, "What did you do in the war, Daddy?" Millions served during the years of the Vietnam War. Some who were drafted and fortunate were sent to serve in Europe. Others remained in the United States. The reality is that even during a war, a significant percentage served in a capacity that did not require them to be in a combat unit or on the front lines of the fighting. Those in support of the men in the direct line of fire outnumbered the men who did the fighting.

Ultimately, for those in B2-7, the question is easy to answer. Every B2-7 soldier who contributed to this work performed courageously and heroically under the worst of circumstances. And, all performed their duties in the face of possible death, not just daily, but hourly and during every minute of each hour. These were not heroic exploits on a sporting field or on an entertainment stage because there is no such thing as a heroic act in those settings. While the men of B2-7 may believe that it was simply doing a job that was expected of them, doing the jobs required putting aside fear, putting aside concerns for their own safety, running to the aid of one of their brothers in arms, risking themselves when bullets were aimed at them, grenades thrown in their direction and other ordnance used against them.

What began as a work to recognize one man is, in fact, a work that recognizes all who contributed to this work. But, in reality, it recognizes all who served in B2-7 as well as the tens of thousands who fought bravely because without all of them working toward one common goal, the outcomes may not have been as successful as they were. Just like a puzzle, some pieces are bigger than others, but all the pieces are necessary to complete the picture. In B2-7, to increase the odds of each man coming home either to a family or to someday have a family, required each man to do what needed to be done. The fact that so many survived is evidence of the extent to which each sacrificed for others.

There's no doubt that Top and McCaffrey were important to the men of B2-7. At the same time, their survival depended upon every other man doing his job as a platoon sergeant, squad leader, point man, machine gunner, ammo bearer, radio operator, medic, forward observer, or whatever responsibility he had.

I've never asked the question posed. A lot can be discerned seeing a soldier in uniform wearing his or her ribbons, but simply seeing the uniform fails to communicate what it takes to earn them. This assumes, of course, that all the awarded medals are represented by the ribbons. That may not always be the case. Anyone who is familiar with military awards can get some idea about a person's military career, regardless of its length, by simply looking at the ribbons on the uniform and the badges and patches that may adorn it. For the sons of 1st Sergeant Trainer, what he wore told an incomplete story.

Over the years, I had seen him in the Class A Dress Green uniform many times with "all" the ribbons, pins, etc. And, even as he approached the day of his retirement from the Army after twenty-one plus years, the uniform never told the full story. It was not until 2006, thirty-five years after he had retired and I was in my fifties that I saw his full display for the first time sitting framed on a desk—in the basement. There was always that effort or attempt to diminish any self-recognition.

The reality was that throughout the years when we lived near relatives in Ohio there were "whispers" about my father being wounded in Korea, but there were never details. But, beyond that, there was nothing more. And, the black and white photos he sent during the first tour in Vietnam supplemented the news coverage, and there did not seem to be anything more that I needed to know.

There were things I learned, perhaps the result of growing up an Army brat, that I took to heart while in the Army myself. There was one important thing that was especially important. To the extent that I could identify anything on a uniform that informed me that someone was a Korean War veteran or had been in Vietnam and in combat, I shied away. I understood that I was serving, but I was not a soldier. I knew and know to this day what a soldier is. I was raised by one. And, he served with men who were either soldiers already or who became soldiers in Vietnam.

More than forty-five years after they first came into contact with each other, the men of B2-7 who regularly get together exhibited their relationship with their Top. Sometimes, an innocuous suggestion said in jest becomes something special and so it was on an evening in July 2014. We gathered at "Camp Gast" as we do every summer. Top, my father, was sitting on the deck of Gast's cabin while the rest of us were sitting by the bonfire. Someone said Top's going to bed. Another suggested that everyone march up and give him a goodnight salute. There was some apprehension about that saluting thing . . . enlisted men saluting enlisted men. Not being in any habit of saluting my father, I decided to hang back and be a spectator for this one. Everyone else lined up and marched from the lakeside toward the cabin's deck. Suddenly, what was said in jest only a few minutes earlier had turned into a moment to be witnessed as a dozen or so old soldiers marched toward that cabin. This was a sign of their respect for their Top. At some point, my father noticed them, and when they stopped, someone gave an order to salute. My father straightened up and returned their salute in the same spirit that they had given theirs. It was a moment to be savored.

Being able to witness those few minutes in 2014 or hearing the men of B2-7 volunteer their stories answered the question I never needed to ask. In doing so, they also answered the question about what they themselves did during the war and what others in B2-7 survived. Together, they had to fight for their lives.

At home, there were no bullets aimed at us and no grenades hurled in our direction. Our sacrifice was his absence. But, it was his presence that may have mattered more as the men of B2-7 were willing to underscore how much more important it was for my father to be with them than at home. And, in their willingness to share with me, they told me how important it was to them that my father was there for them. And, for that, I am the fortunate son.

GENERAL BARRY MCCAFFREY (RET.) & 1ST SGT. EMERSON TRAINER (RET.)
Picture taken in 2000

Top's "Secret" Army Awards prominently displayed in the basement.

MEN OF DIVISION, (B2-7)

Dale Beierman

Paul Decker

Rich Dorsey

Gerald "Jerry" Gast

Now . . .

Edd Holtz and Jesse "Pops" Groves

Fred Hall

Jack Jeter

Men of Division, (B2-7)

Jon "Snag" Johnson

Michael K McMahan

Jack "Squirt" Miller

William "Bill" Montgomery

Now . . .

Chris Sayre   Larry "Skinny" Spaulding

Author Timothy Trainer

Basic Training '72

Camp Gast 2015

ABOUT THE AUTHOR

Tim Trainer is an army brat. He was born into the Army in Japan and was a high school junior when his father retired from the Army. Typical of Army or military brats of the times, he had attended ten schools by the time of his high school graduation.

He did not arrive in the United States until he was past his fifth birthday. After arriving in the United States, the Army life meant living in various parts of the United States, on and off post, depending upon his father's duty station.

He had three "tours of duty" at Ft. Knox, KY, (some elementary school, some high school, and basic training). Upon his discharge from the Army in July 1975, he left the Army behind permanently. At the time of his discharge, he was twenty-one and half years old but had spent twenty years as either an army brat or on active duty.

After the Army years, he eventually earned a law degree and moved to the Washington, D.C., area in 1987. Since moving to the Washington, D.C., area, he has worked as an attorney in federal government agencies and in the private sector. He has traveled extensively around the world, including several trips to Vietnam.

This work is evidence that his break from the Army was not "permanent." In the late 1990s, his father, who was reuniting regularly with men he had served with in B2-7, invited him to meet the guys when they met in Washington, D.C. This led to his father's invitation to attend a summer reunion in 2003. Since 2003, Mr. Trainer has been a regular attendee of the B2-7 reunions in Washington, D.C., and at the summer gatherings at what he calls "Camp Gast."

CPSIA information can be obtained
at www.ICGtesting.com
Printed in the USA
BVOW09*1252250517
484966BV00001B/2/P